ENDORSEMENTS

"This book offers the most positive, realistic, uplifting
approach to stress I have ever read. The most important factor of all
is that the principles explained here will work for you."
True achievers are driven by a power which is greater than they are.
A power so deep within their minds they are possibly unaware that it is
their driving force."

Ms. Mary Lou Adonizio, Director
Institute for Research and Community Services
and Continuing Education
Edinboro University of Pennsylvania

"Dr. Webb and Dr. Holmes show incredible insight
and rich understanding in their ability to turn stress
into a positive force in our lives. This is a real breakthrough
into positive empowering energy."

Ms. Mary E. Bjustrom, Business Manager
The Advanced Technology Center
The Boeing Company

"It is so very positive to see such a vision of hope for ourselves
and the world around us. Dr. Holmes and Dr. Webb provide powerful
and creative concepts that offer the potential to transform
both our internal and external environments
into a higher plane of human development."

Dr. Claude Zahar, Director
Family Advocacy
U.S. Army, Fort Ritchie

D0318004

THE
POSITIVE STRESS
FACTOR

THE POSITIVE STRESS FACTOR

Rebecca Jo Holmes
Mary Lee Webb

LEE ROSS PUBLISHING

Energy Dynamics[R] is a registered trademark of Dr. Rebecca Jo Holmes.

Cover design by GFC Graphics. Glenn Frederick Cassel & Lucille Cassel.

Library of Congress Cataloging in Publication Data:

Holmes, Rebecca Jo and Mary Lee Webb.
    The positive stress factor

        ISBN 0-9634383-7-9
        1. Business   2. Self-improvement

Printed in the United States of America   92-61682

We dedicate this book

to the men who gave inspiration to our lives:

Reuben Ross Holmes
John Lee Webb
Marcel Joseph Vogel

and the women who gave life to the inspiration:

Helen Derco Holmes
Marie Rosenau Webb

CONTENTS

ACKNOWLEDGEMENTS

PREFACE

O N E : THE POWER OF SILENCE
Page 1

How do you communicate?
What do you say with silence?
How can you turn "transitions" into powerful experiences?

T W O : THE POWER OF HUMAN ENERGY
Page 7

How can you unleash the power of emotion?
Can emotional energy be focused into a positive power?
Why is the energy of emotion so powerful?

T H R E E : THE POWER OF POSITIVE STRESS
Page 25

Why does stress always seem to be negative?
Why does the power of stress paralyze you?
How can you turn stress into a positive opportunity?

F O U R : THE POWER OF ENERGY DYNAMICS^{R}
Page 44

What is so dynamic about energy?
How does your interaction with other people become powerful?
How can interpersonal dynamics be used positively?

F I V E : THE POWER OF PHYSICAL ENERGY
Page 65

What does nutrition have to do with energy?
How do you convert physical energy into power?
What effect does food have on your emotional power?

S I X : THE POWER OF MEMORY
Page 85

Where is your memory?
What are the impressions which trigger your reactions?
How does positive stress open the door to change?

S E V E N : THE POWER OF SELF-ESTEEM
Page 108

Why is self-esteem such an elusive quality?
Who builds your power?
How can stress be a springboard to self-esteem?

E I G H T : THE POWER OF THE 21ST CENTURY MIND
Page 133

Are you ready for the 21st century?
Who are those who can lead into the next millenium?
Where does the power of stress belong in the next century?

EPILOGUE

INDEX

BIBLIOGRAPHY

ACKNOWLEDGEMENTS

No book is ever written, edited, designed, or published in a vacuum. The hours, minutes, and days of our lives are filled with the encouragement, support, and love of many who have sacrificed for us, who have learned with us, and who have been our confidantes.

A group of dedicated people spent many hours with us over the years to bring this work to you. Their efforts kept us going through the years of triumphs, disappointments, successes, and disasters. The stuff of which life is made!

We thank Phyllis who has been an anchor in our storm, Elizabeth who has been the ship's rudder, Linda who has given us the wind for our sails, Jeanne who has steered us to new ports, and Malinda who has taught us about reefs and sinkholes.

We thank Mary Lou who never loses sight of the dream and who always searches for new directions. Fred, Lucille, Joey, and Jay are the touchstones of our progress. We acknowledge the contributions of those who by their deeds taught us lessons in tolerance, in perseverance, and in our own intuitive sense of right and wrong.

The personal friends are always there as only true friends can be. Mary, Sara, Bobbie, and Hilda are those treasured friends of a lifetime. There is a special place for "Buddy".

We thank the clients over the years whose stories are here for you to read. Their stories breathe life into THE POSITIVE STRESS FACTOR and we celebrate their successes.

No one learns only from success. The failures and disappointments of each lifetime teach us all. Those who have criticized and discouraged us deserve our thanks, too. Without them, we would not learn the lesson of our own dedication to the truth. We acknowledge all of our teachers.

We must also thank you, the reader, who by purchasing THE POSITIVE STRESS FACTOR, has changed your life . . . and ours.

PREFACE

This is a book about *energy*. This is a book about *potential*. It is also a book about discovery. THE POSITIVE STRESS FACTOR is a book about *your own goals and your own aspirations* which are so very similar to all of us who want more, who want success, and who want life to be an adventure.

An adventure starts with a dream, but the dream cannot become reality without the energy which propels it. Your adventure might be starting a new business, developing a new relationship, facing a new job, or creating a new vision. Whatever it is, it takes energy to get there and to make it happen! Energy to live and energy to make the living sparkle with possiblity.

This book was not written as a self-help manual with rules for living. It was not written as a step-by-step handbook for success. *You have to take what is here and write your own handbook for success.* All through this book you are given experiences and ideas. You have to breathe life into these ideas and make them your own guides.

Over the years, the two of us have shared these ideas with business owners, entrepreneurs, managers, teachers, sales professionals, and hundreds of other successful people who wanted more energy in their lives and wanted to achieve greater goals. Out of their achievements with Energy Dynamics^R we have carved a book for you. It only scratches the surface of what you can achieve. It is a beginning to find the answers to obstacles we all face in our lifetimes. Fear. Stress. Misunderstanding. Lack of self-confidence. Lack of self-esteem. Lack of power.

We do not expect to answer all of your questions, but we do expect that you will think about the possibilities here. The book begins and ends with one truth. Life is a dynamic journey and sometimes the most fearful part of it is a transition. Facing that fearful transition in life brings everything else into focus. Life is about learning, growing, and being. Energy Dynamics^R is the breath of that life.

*"True silence is the rest of the mind;
it is to the spirit what sleep is to the body,
nourishment and refreshment."*

William Penn

ONE

THE POWER OF SILENCE

My father was dying. I watched his face as a respirator breathed life into him. I watched his chest move up and down and thought about how I never noticed that movement until now. He had been breathing all of his life, but I never noticed before. Until now.

My father was dying. I listened to the wheezing sound of the respirator and watched the flashing lights of the cardiac monitor as it measured out his life in micro-seconds and disembodied bleeps. As I listened, I tried hard to remember the sound of his voice. I had heard that voice for forty years and I was desperately trying to remember it now.

My father was dying. All of my life, he had been there, supporting and caring for me. All of my life, he had laughed and smiled. All of my life, he was a reality. Now, the reality was changing. *"All of my life"* would change, too. When a spouse dies, the survivor has some memories which do not involve the missing person. But, when a parent dies, the child is left with no memory of life without that parent. My life was to be forever changed by this event, and I had no power over it.

He had no power either. His life was not under his control. He was a slave to the respirator which gave him breath, but robbed him of his identity. My father loved to talk and he talked to strangers

1

and friends equally well. He constantly retold stories about his life. He recounted stories about being at the great battles of World War II. North Africa. Anzio. Stories about the beautiful Hartz Mountains in Germany and the golden-haired girls among the yellow canaries not far from Berchtesgaden. He retold the events of his life as if he were narrating a movie. He recalled small details and related each of those details with great precision. But now, if he could recall those details, he could not speak of them.

What was he thinking? This man who always told us everything he was thinking. Even if we did not want to hear it! What were the words he would have spoken had he the chance? As I watched this silent man, I couldn't help but think how unfair this ending was for him. A man who lived by the miracle of speech would die with none. A man who loved to use his voice to control, cajole, and manipulate could use his voice for nothing. He had been robbed. He was helpless.

But, a strange thing happened during the months he lay silent. Those around him rallied and communicated with him perhaps more than ever before. His wife discovered that she could communicate with him through touch or a lifted eyebrow at the appropriate moment. In his silence, he had somehow become more empowered as the days wore on. I realized that he understood far more than I thought he could. He was dying, but he was more "alive" than at any other time in his life.

The stress of watching helplessly while someone you love dies is monstrous. For those who have not experienced the death of a loved one, words cannot explain the feelings you have. You feel as though you are in a movie for which you have no script. Everything you have known before, takes on a different meaning. Everything you do is mechanical and unimportant. Your world is turned upside down and you feel out of control.

In the last hours of my father's life, he laughed. We could not hear the sound of that laugh, but we could "see" it in his eyes. That laugh was probably one of best I ever "heard" from him. It certainly is the most memorable. My father's eyes were bright blue and twinkled with life. As little more than a shell, he looked like a powerful man lying there laughing at something we had said.

My father was dying. As I watched his death, I felt the power of the man. This silent man used his last bit of energy to laugh with me and then, he was gone. His death was a great learning for me, as well as those around me. He taught me that there is an energy of emotion which does not depend on speech. Power does not come from speech either. His power came from using the stress of his situation in a positive way. He taught me that life is dynamic and changing. There is a power that comes from using that dynamic life.

The power of his silence was the "positive stress factor." His impact on those around him, family, friends, nurses, and doctors was a magnificent example of the impact of one "energy system" on others. In silence, he taught me much more than he ever could with words.

His name was Reuben Ross Holmes, and I am proud to be his daughter, Rebecca.

THE POSITIVE STRESS FACTOR

In the following pages, you will be challenged to think of stress in a new way. You will be asked to examine some of your ideas about stress and power. You will be introduced to new and old concepts. Most of all, you will be given something about which to think. That is precisely what we intend. We intend that you think. We want this book to be an adventure for you.

The ideas here are just that--ideas about a future you could have. We want you to rethink your ideas about stress and come up with your own plan for change instead of following someone else's rules for living. You can begin by thinking of yourself as an "energy system." Your energy system can have its own set of rules. You can change your stress into a positive power in your life by taking control and empowering yourself. Stress is not the last step in the process. It is the first!

THE POSITIVE STRESS FACTOR is the result of years of research into the impact of stress on the entire physical, mental, and emotional system of an individual. The pages of this book are filled with the stories of real people. These real people have private lives, but many of them wanted their stories told because they knew that the information would be valuable for others. We owe a debt of gratitude to these clients and friends who have explored their own stresses with us and shared those experiences with you.

These people are those who have succeeded and those who have failed. They have either looked for challenges or had challenges thrust upon them. They are ordinary people and extraordinary people who share one thing. They all share stress. They all share that ability to use that stress is a positive way. They all share the capacity to learn and to change. You could have that same capacity and the opportunity to use the stress in your life in a positive way. It's up to you.

This book resulted because people wanted to know how to turn stress around. It was also the result of our desire to share the knowledge we have about psychological and physical stress and how to use those stresses to your advantage.

Dr. Holmes developed a method to use stress more positively by using the energy system we all have to make positive changes. Energy Dynamics^R is a way to get to the bottom of the physical, emotional, and mental components which complicate physical stresses. Dr. Webb began to work with her to blend the power of psychological theory to this program. It is that blend of the physical and the psychological that makes Energy Dynamics^R so valuable to you. It may be the first time you have actually felt that you are a completely integrated system of *body and mind*.

We are presenting these ideas to you as we would if we were speaking directly to you because these concepts have their beginnings with each individual. It is through the personal and informal format of this book that we hope to give you some new thoughts about some old subjects. Some of our written language is very informal and more "verbal" than "written". We had a reason for this; we wanted to "speak" to you rather than "write" to you. As you travel through THE POSITIVE STRESS FACTOR, listen to the words, don't just "read" them.

All through the book, we have included little assignments for you just as if you were in one of our seminars or sessions. These exercises or experiences are important for many reasons. We have learned over the years that experience is not only a great teacher, it is also fun! Without direct experiences, much of the information is academic and impractical. Make this book practical for yourself. Use it and learn from it.

ENERGY DYNAMICS^R AND POSITIVE STRESS

Energy Dynamics^R is not the only subject of this book. It is one tool we use to harness stress and make that stress positive in our lives. The idea behind Energy Dynamics^R is that some of us can unlock our potential and some of us can become more successful in our careers, professions, and our relationships with others. The person who can use the information in THE POSITIVE STRESS FACTOR is the person who has already reached a level of achievement beyond the ordinary.

We believe that Energy Dynamics^R can change your life. As a matter of fact, we intended to title this book, BUY THIS BOOK, IT WILL CHANGE YOUR LIFE! Using stress as a positive force in your life is a powerful new thought, but it can well be a very successful one. We teach Energy Dynamics^R every year to owners of businesses, career professionals, executive managers, university administrators, as well as armed forces personnel, middle managers, and human resource directors. These men and women and others like them are on the cutting edge of leadership and achievement. They face challenges every day, and not only do they survive, they also share something intangible about leadership that we feel can be better understood and used through Energy Dynamics^R than through anything else.

The important thing about this approach is that it has worked well with achievers of all ages, each sex, and many walks of life. Because we are blending the physical, mental, and emotional elements of the energy system, we can begin to use more than just a portion of our personal power for success.

Remember that Energy Dynamics[R] is one of many approaches to personal stress. It may or may not be the only one for you. As you read the following pages, we want you to think about the ideas presented here. If you can answer "yes" to the following questions, you have chosen the right book to read. *Are you under any stress today?* Were you under any stress in the past? *Do you want to enjoy life?* Do you want to get out of life as much as you can? *Do you want more power over your life?* Are you ready for a new adventure?

Turn the page.

"*Thus only can you gain the secret isolated joy of the thinker,*
who knows that, a hundred years
after he is dead and forgotten,
men who never heard of him
will be moving to the measure of his thought--
the subtle rapture of a postponed power,
which the world knows not
because it has no external trappings,
but which to his prophetic vision is more real than that
which commands an army."

Oliver Wendell Holmes, Jr.

T W O

THE POWER OF HUMAN ENERGY

Mark Twain is quoted as saying, "Thunder is good, thunder is impressive; but it is lightning that does the work." Energy is like lightning. It takes energy to get the work done. As any good coach will tell us, "All of us can talk a good game, but it takes energy to get the ball over the goal line."

ENERGY AND POWER

Imagine a power plant which generates electricity. The power plant takes in fuel to be converted into electricity through a series of transformations which are beyond the understanding of most of us. Engineers know the process. We don't have to because we depend on them to get the electricity to us. We don't have to know the process to enjoy the power that electricity brings to our lives. Likewise, we don't have to understand the inner workings of our bodies and minds to enjoy the power that our internal energy gives us.

The power plant uses fuel much like we use food, water, and oxygen. These fuels are converted into different types of energy and then we use that energy again. The food we eat, the water we drink,

7

and even the thoughts we think are the fuels we use every day to make our own "internal electricity" and power. Our "power plant" is the human energy system which generates other forms of energy just like the electrical power plant does.

The human energy system takes in the fuel we give it and makes new forms of energy. It takes the food, burns it through digestion, and in the process, makes heat energy which keeps us warm. It also converts food energy into other types of energy such as chemical energy which helps us to move and think. The chemical energy creates new body cells and tissues from this transformation of energy.

The human energy system does something that the electric power plant does not. *The power plant does not think independent thoughts.* The power plant does not create anything which has not been created before without instructions from its engineers. The engineers have the creative power to change the system. The power plant cannot do what the human energy system can do. It cannot interpret its own power and make decisions about how to use it. The power plant must be told what to do every step of the way. The power plant does not think about its place in the world or have a personal values system. These are unique to the *human* energy system.

The analogy to the power plant is very simple. The reality of the human energy system is far more complex. The explanations of the inner workings of the system are too complicated for us to explore here, but it is important to know that there is a reason for these rather complicated instructions on basic physiology. We want you to think of yourself as a little power plant with all of the basic capabilities we described here, but do not stop there. Use your capabilities to go beyond the basics into the extraordinary. Use your own mind to explore this energy of your own system.

Let's take some time out here for something we call a "think bite." You have heard of "sound bites" used on television so often these days. Those are little excerpts from speeches used on the evening news programs. They are specially designed to give you, the listener and viewer, a certain perspective on the news that straight news reporting won't do.

In our case, we'd like to call these little interruptions "think bites" for a very good reason. We want you to think while you're reading. Not too much. Just a little. Part of what we ask clients to do in sessions or in seminars is to take what they have just heard and explore it for themselves. So, here is your first "think bite."

Think Bite #1

Let's experiment with breathing. You remember breathing, don't you? You do it every day. Several hundred times a day. Breathing is one of the functions we do so automatically that we don't realize how vital it is until we cannot do it.

One of the fuels the human energy system uses for energy and power is breath. The deeper you breathe and the more effectively you use your breath, the better the energy flow will be in your system. We have all had lectures about standing up straight and breathing from the diaphragm. We all know that oxygen and carbon dioxide exhange in our lungs so that we can live. But, the breathing process itself is something which involves more than just gaseous exchange. The cycle of breathing is important because it is balanced. It is totally balanced. Just try this experiment.

Breathe in deeply. Now, without pausing, breathe in again. Without exhaling. Can't do it, can you? Breathing *in* must be followed by breathing *out*. There is a natural balance to the breath cycle. In and out. Another important part of the breath cycle is the *pause* in between the inhalation and the exhalation. You cannot go directly from inhale to exhale without *pausing*. Try it.

Have you ever sat on a beach or near a beach and listened to the waves coming in to the shore? For many of us, it is one of the most soothing and pleasant sounds on earth. The steady balanced cycle of "in and out." That's probably why so many people love to sit on the beach or walk on the beach. The relaxing motion of the waves and the steady cycle of the water exchange. People often say they rest and sleep better near the ocean than anywhere else. Even just listening to the steady wind lulls us to sleep. The importance of the cycle is in the balance.

Try something right now. Take a deep breath. As deeply as you can. Fill up your lungs. Hold it a second or two and then breathe out as completely as you can. How deeply can you breathe? Do your shoulders move when you inhale? Those of you who have been in choirs or have sung solo know that the sight of shoulders rising and falling is a "no-no!" You must breathe from the diaphragm.

Try this. Hold your hand on your stomach right below your rib cage. As you breathe in, imagine that you are filling a giant balloon in your chest cavity. When you blow up a balloon, you see air fill the bottom of the balloon first, don't you? Imagine as you breathe in that the bottom of your chest cavity or your stomach fills first. Feel your hand move "out" as you breathe "in."

If you have a buddy with you, have him or her hold a hand over your stomach and try this experiment again.

Keep trying to breathe deeply enough to move his or her hand out. When a vocal teacher tries to get students to breathe deeply from the diaphragm, he or she has the student lie on the floor with a book on the stomach. As the student breathes in, the book should rise.

When you breathe in, think about the air coming into your system not just as a necessary process, but as a balanced cycle bringing new energy into your system. Just sit now for a few minutes and breathe in and out thinking about what you just read. Watch out for hyperventilation. Breathe deeply and slowly. Not too many breaths at a time so that you become dizzy.

The word "energy" has many meanings to many people. It might be important for us to define the word before we use it any further. The word has come to have meanings which go far beyond what Webster ever imagined. For the sake of our discussions in THE POSITIVE STRESS FACTOR, let's look at the meaning which we place on the word.

WHAT IS ENERGY?

Energy can be defined as "drive," "enthusiasm," "vigor," "power," and "vitality." S. I. Hayakawa uses the word energy as a synonym for "zest" and "gusto." Webster defines "energy," as "vitality of expression" and "vigor in performance." The energy we speak of here is the energy Frederick Harmon discusses in THE EXECUTIVE ODYSSEY. Mr. Harmon believes that "the higher the aspiration . . . the greater the energy released." We believe that the more positive the use of that energy, "the greater the power to propel the individual forward in life." (Harmon, page 41)

Over the past ten years, we have explored this energy and the energy system with people just like you who have led lives of achievement and success, but who have had some experiences with stress. These people have used their stress as the key to unlock their own personal power and strength. The great Sir Laurence Olivier urged his fellow actors to "use your weaknesses; aspire to your strengths." Just as Mr. Harmon suggests, the greater the aspiration to achieve, the greater the use of this energy and the greater the power in our lives.

The energy of positive stress is energy which is vital, powerful, and vigorous. Two pioneers in wellness and stress reduction are Dr. John Travis and Regina Sara Ryan. Their WELLNESS WORKBOOK is a benchmark for those who want to find, not just a remedy for a "sick" life, but rather a guidepost for a "well" life. They discuss energy in many aspects of life including work, creativity, relationships, and thinking. "Thinking is a form of electrochemical energy generated in the brain. Thinking is an energy output form. . . and relies heavily on the energy of emotions in creating its internal maps of external reality." (Travis and Ryan, page 128) The *energy of emotions* is one aspect of positive stress in our lives. It is this energy we can use to turn a stressful situation into an opportunity for change and success. You can blend physical, mental, and *emotional energy* to direct your own personal power.

WHAT IS DYNAMIC ABOUT ENERGY?

Webster defines the word "dynamic" as "relating to energy; marked by continuous, productive activity or change." This dynamic component moves energy around and causes change to take place constantly. We look at the individual as an energy system that works as a whole to think, walk, talk, and feel. Think about this human energy system as that complex power plant which can be monitored, changed, and enhanced continuously to make your life the most productive it can be.

One of our favorite quotes is one from Ellen Degeneria. "My grandmother started walking five miles a day when she was sixty. She's ninety-five today and we don't know where the hell she is." It is not enough to feel the energy, you have to use it for some purpose. The energy to use what you learn must be focused in some way so that the power of that energy can be released. The dynamic use of the energy which comes from stress directs our living and many times gives new meaning to everything we do.

We both spent time teaching high school English in our earlier lives. Mary Lee learned after one year that this could not be her life's work. It took Rebecca eight years to discover the same thing. We both learned one thing from those experiences. You can "lead a horse to water . . " You know the rest. Some students have an energy which practically knocks you over with its enthusiasm.

Others are constantly "bored" by school, by their teachers, by life, in general.

Even without our conscious intervention, the system is dynamic. It does change and sometimes those changes are extremely dramatic.

POSITIVE STRESS AND ENERGY DYNAMICS[R]

The development of Energy Dynamics[R] came after discovery upon discovery over a long period of time. But, the dynamics of the energy system had been explored for many, many years before we began. It will continue long after we are gone. The research into transformational systems and the exploration of the human energy system will continue to expand for many years as we learn more and more about ourselves and the possibilities we all have.

Our exploration of the energy system began over 12 years ago. As with most projects, the beginning and the ending do not seem to have very much in common. The beginning was based on personal exploration. It was only after we made discoveries about our own personal lives, that we each began to adapt what we had learned to our professions. The use of energy in both physical medicine and in psychology is well documented. We can list the pioneers who first approached these fields with an eye on the energy system. Pioneers like Carl Jung, Hans Selye, Fritz Perls, Dolores Kreiger, Marcel Vogel, Major Bertrand DeJarnette, and a hundred others asked probing questions about human energy systems.

Jung described the personality types which seem to be dominated by the particular use of energy within the individual's system. Selye explored stress and its impact on the human system in many ways. Perls worked with the energy system and the "gestalt" or whole of emotional and mental life. Kreiger taught nurses and other health care providers the power of human touch and the energy of healing. Vogel examined the intangible communication of plants and the relationship between that communication and the human energy system. DeJarnette worked with energy in the physical body and the intricate balancing act of muscles, bones, and the nervous system. All of these explorers worked with the energy system in its various forms in an effort to explain the dynamics of life.

Energy, some physicists say, is one of only two realities. The other reality is matter. If all that we can see, all that is tangible, is matter, then, that which we cannot see, is energy. Energy in its many forms is the powerful force behind the movement and manipulation of matter. Without going into great physiological detail, the reality of energy and its impact on physical matter gives us life. The dynamic changes of that energy give us the variety of life. With an understanding of those dynamics, we can make conscious use of the energy system.

THE ENERGY OF COMMUNICATION

The work of Marcel Vogel led us into an exploration of the dynamics of energy and it is to Marcel that we are indebted for supporting our work. In THE SECRET LIFE OF PLANTS, Thompkins and Bird describe the work of Vogel and other scientists of the day. Their work centered on the dynamics of plant communication pathways.

In their experiments, which stand today as breakthroughs in communication studies, Vogel and his assistants discovered that there was an energy which caused the communication to occur between plant life. Not only did this energy allow for communication on that level, but he and his fellow scientists also believed that this energy could be used by human beings to communicate more effectively.

Vogel believed that "his research with plants (could) help man to the recognition of long-ignored truths . . .(Vogel) believes he can teach children to release their emotions and watch the effects in a measurable way." (Thompkins and Bird, page 18) As a matter of fact, Marcel loved to work with children on experiments and did many programs for public television with children. He explained that the

14

joy of working with children came from the fact that there were no inhibitions to learning and exploring. Children have a sense that nothing is impossible. Everything can be done once you learn *how to do it.* Adults, on the other hand, bring to new experiences all of the old impressions and inhibitions which prevent true learning. There is a wonderful expression about true learning. "A mind is like a parachute, it only works when open."

Vogel believed that children and adults could learn "the art of loving and know truly that when they think a thought, they release a tremendous power... By knowing that *they are their thoughts,* they will know how to use thinking to achieve . . . emotional and intellectual growth." (Thompkins and Bird, page 18)

The importance of unreleased energy and stress was very much a part of Vogel's work as well. "So much of the ills and suffering in life come from our inability to release stresses and forces within us. When a person rejects us, we rebel inside . . . This builds up a stress . . . which depletes the body energy." (Thompkins and Bird, page 32)

In a personal conversation with Marcel, one of many in the years we knew him, he talked about emotion. "An emotion is an energy pattern, a response to a stimulus. When I squeeze your hand, you feel the warmth of my hand and pressure. Beyond the pressure and the warmth of my hand is a feeling that transcends physical matter. This gives us two realities, the physical and the emotional. The physical is matter and the emotional is energy."

Marcel's last conversation with us, just a few weeks before his death, centered on the importance of understanding emotional energy. His concern was that those who explored the energy system did not fully recognize that the energy of the system was powerful and that the impressions of experiences on the system had far reaching effects.

Energy as a study was Marcel Vogel's life work. It was a labor of love. His focus was finding answers to age old questions. He was a good and dear friend who is greatly missed. What is not missing is the power with which he touched those who knew him and who continue his work.

The dynamics of energy and the ways in which we can use that energy for our own empowerment is the story of Ann. Ann was a woman who had suffered for years with cancer which had threatened to kill her many times. She was a strong and bright woman who cared so much for family and friends that her illness took a backseat to their needs. She had fought off the cancer through two severe episodes and she was beginning another episode when she came to see us. Ann was well along in her exploration of her own self-worth and she *could not believe* that with so much to live for, she was to be challenged with her mortality again. She had begun classes at the university. Her children were well on their way to independence. She was finally becoming her own person in many ways. Then, the bell tolled.

Ann approached her recurrence of cancer very differently than she had in the past. For one thing, she did not take the doctors' pronouncements as law. She wanted to explore the possibilities that perhaps the cancer could be destroyed by other means than the conventional. Ann had done the chemotherapy to no avail. She had been treated with radiation many times. What the doctors said would not happen, happened. The cancer returned. Ann felt there was no more point to using unsuccessful treatments She wanted to try something else. If she was to die, she wanted it to be on her own terms.

The energy she expended in fighting the cancer on her own terms was hard to come by. She not only had to fight the cancer, she had to fight her family and friends who thought she was making a big mistake in refusing the conventional treatments. Ann began her exploration with the cancer by exploring her emotional reactions to it.

Her first reaction was the natural reaction of fear. The energy of that fear caused her to be irritable with her husband. The energy of the fear caused her to withdraw from her friends. That same

16

energy reminded her of other fears. One fear was that if she died, her family, husband, and children could not survive without her. In her past experiences, she had felt cut off from those who had died. Ann had never accepted the fact that when someone you loved died, the love continued in some way.

Ann's church had been of little comfort to her with these questions. She resented the fact that the church could not comfort her. Her fears were real and she wanted answers. Through her sessions in Energy Dynamics[R], Ann learned that the deaths she had experienced in the past were painful, not because of the separation from the loved one, but because of her own unwillingness to move on with her life.

Ann worked through most of those experiences with death, but the major exploration she had yet to complete was done in her final sessions. Ann faced her anger. With whom was she angry? The cancer? Her family? Her church? Or? She was angry with the one she felt was responsible for her death. Call that someone God or Ann herself. Ann didn't really separate the two at that point. She was dying and she was mad about it. Ann had accepted her death. She just wanted someone to know how angry she was. She felt there was a problem with that. Her church taught her that she should not be angry with God. But, here was the conflict. She was angry. She was mad as Hell! She had to release that anger in some way.

She did. The confrontation she had was private and we did not intrude upon it. We will respect her privacy once again by not even speculating about the energy she released. She did it by herself. After the session together, she headed off for a holiday weekend with her family. That was the last time we saw Ann alive. Ten days later, she was gone.

Ann had lunch with a friend of hers a few days after her last session with us and her friend asked her how it was going. Ann reportedly said, "Fine, I've taken care of everything." Evidently she had. Her husband told us at the funeral that the doctors felt that the cancer had not in fact caused her death. Her heart just stopped. And she was gone.

17

Ann taught us a great lesson. Each person's individual energy is a private matter to be shared if he or she chooses. We are telling you the story of Ann because she told us to do so. She wanted others to learn something from her life and mostly, from her death. She was a grand lady who was one of the most brilliant examples of self-esteem and empowerment we have ever seen. She had made her own decisions and used the time she had to her best advantage. She cleared away, not only her own personal questions, but issues with her extended family, husband, and children. She chose her life and her death with dignity and clear purpose.

There is one side note to the story of Ann. There was no sadness for us at her death. Like others who loved her, we miss her. We miss her smile and her great sense of humor. We miss her uncompromising spirit and her stamina. We also miss her courage and the inspiration she left behind. But, unlike some others, we knew she had made her own decisions. As we were leaving the clinic one day, an acquaintance of Ann's who did not know the whole story said to us, "It's too bad you couldn't help her," implying that by dying she had failed. The message was "if she died, she failed . . . and you did, too." Neither of us, nor, we are sure, Ann herself, felt she failed. She succeeded in the best way possible. She was an empowered woman. She was a dynamic energy system exhibiting a great self-esteem. She was a positive force among those she touched. She will live forever. Vogel would have said, "Now, you know." He always liked to have you learn your own lessons and then have him affirm them for you. He would have been pleased to know that like the children with whom he loved to work, Ann had released a tremendous power by releasing the energy of her emotion. If we learn from that release of energy, then that experience is powerful. Perhaps it is the most powerful use of energy we know.

Sometimes, the release of the energy of emotion is not easy. Our impressions from the past and the experiences we have had with others often cause such a shield of protection for us, that showing any emotion is difficult, if not totally impossible.

THE BLOCKING OF EMOTIONAL ENERGY

Colleen is a marketing director for a major hotel group who for years has struggled with the emotional energy she sees others release from time to time. She is overwhelmed by the emotions she witnesses. She describes the feeling as if she is being smothered with energy from the other person. Because that energy is so powerful for her, Colleen withdraws from it terrified. It is not the actual emotion which frightens her, it is the "energy" of the emotion.

This release of energy frightens Colleen so much that she says she cannot really "hear" what the other person is saying. She herself withdraws from her own emotions the same way. When we asked her why she does this, Colleen explained that, when she was young, her father often would come home from work and vent his anger with his wife and children. He would not listen to anyone else's thoughts or feelings. Because he was under such pressure at his job, he could think of nothing else but his own problems.

As a consequence, over the years Colleen learned to withdraw and actually escape from this outpouring of emotional energy. Colleen found a place within herself where she was safe, and she stayed there rather than risk causing more emotional outbursts from her father. Her energy system learned to adapt to the uncontrolled emotional energy she witnessed as a child by shrinking from any emotional energy release herself.

Many people over the years have described for us how they found a secret place within themselves where they were safe. Abused children often escape into fantasy to avoid the emotional tirades of the adults around them. As a matter of fact, current theories of a condition called "Multiple Personality Disorder" support the idea that because of the violent abuse some suffer as children, the identity actually splits itself into many personalities in order to survive.

Fortunately, most of us do not suffer the extreme results of such abuse, but even our small abuses as children cause us to react and behave in specific ways. Colleen is dismayed and appalled at overt emotional reactions. She will not allow herself to express any strong emotion because the energy of those emotions frightened her as a child. As a child, she had no power to change those around her. She could only change herself. She had the power to escape into herself. She protected herself by aborting her own emotional energy. But, as an adult, Colleen has learned that emotional energy is not always a dangerous or frightening thing. As an adult, she has the power to use that emotion positively. The stresses she feels when some emotion surfaces for her can be used positively. From the positive use of that stress and pressure, she has gained new power.

HOW DO WE USE THE ENERGY OF EMOTION?

You are probably asking right about now, "Well, just how did she do that? I understand the idea about the energy system and I know that I'm not just a mass of disconnected thought patterns. But, where do I go from here?" During our research into this energy system, we discovered that each individual gathers information, processes information, and uses information in unique ways based on energy use. The individual systems seem to use information in certain patterns that are not just physical or mental, but that are combinations of both factors.

Many psychological and physical evaluations measure how a person uses physical or mental energy, but when the two are combined, there is an interesting pattern which emerges. Each energy "style" can be identified and used to coach the individual to use stress in positive ways.

In our research, we have correlated many other theories of personality styles and instruments designed to measure styles. The Myers-Briggs Type Indicator™, for example, has been used for years by individuals and businesses to identify the differing styles with which individuals learn and act at work and in their personal lives.

Other psychological studies and testing instruments explore the differences among persons with regard to predispositions and habits. From all of these various studies an understanding has emerged which basically says that we all react differently to the same situations and we all have different methods with which to deal with our worlds.

Many studies in psychology are time-tested and valued by many therapists and their clients for their clinical application. Likewise, the use of these "typing" profiles has revolutionized business management and organizational development programs, but we felt there was more to identifying styles than merely the mental and emotional preferences of people. We began to blend the physical predispositions and preferences of individuals with these psychological studies and found that energy was the key.

Styles based on the use of emotional and physical energy can be defined as combinations of preferences and reactions. Each individual uses his or her energy system differently, not just physically, but also mentally and emotionally. The foundation of the preferences seems to be the patterns of that person's use of energy in all situations. For instance, you may be a person who notices every little change in your physical body. You may be very aware of sensations in your physical system which others never seem to notice. You may be very sensitive to temperature changes and food choices. You may be what Dr. Bernie Seigel calls a "bad patient" who tells your doctor *everything* that is happening to you.

We have found that a person with that style also has some definite personality preferences. A person like that usually is also sensitive to emotional changes and reacts with quick mood shifts. Some doctors call these people "neurotic" or "hypochondriacs," but if you understand that such a person is working out of an energy system which requires that particular kind of emotional, physical, and mental stimulation, then we can give a person like that tools to use stress very positively.

Through Energy Dynamics^R each person can identify the "style" with which he or she reacts to various challenges or stresses, not just emotionally, but physically and mentally as well. In coaching sessions, an individual can use that style to retrace events and impressions from the past to understand the style itself. These events, from memory, are not changed through Energy Dynamics[R] but they are understood more clearly and *used to change our reactions to similar situations! It is this "clearing" process which gives the individual an insight into how to harness stress, alter reactions to situations, and make those stresses positive.*

PATTERNS OF ENERGY AND STRESS

The same tools do not work for each of us in the same way. The ways in which we individually process energy reflect how each of us will react to stress. In his book, NEW WORLD NEW MIND, Dr. Robert Ornstein discusses the new dimensions he feels we must all explore to change the destructive patterns of the 20th century and bring about new paradigms for the 21st century.

Dr. Ornstein and Dr. Paul Erhlich turn their attention to the recent explosion in the self-help field and the proliferation of seminars and programs for personal growth during the last few years. They say, "not everyone needs to meditate, not everyone needs to calm down, not everyone needs to turn off his or her rational thought processes every day." (Ornstein and Erhlich, page 148)

The purpose of THE POSITIVE STRESS FACTOR and this program called Energy Dynamics[R] is just that. *Not everyone should approach stress in exactly the same way.* Each person has a unique energy system and a unique way to process that emotional, physical, and mental energy. Through identifying the styles of each of us, we can work within those styles instead of against them.

Oliver Wendell Holmes said, "What lies behind us and what lies before us are tiny matters compared to what lies within us." The energy which lies within us all can be used in many ways, but the most dynamic way is in the positive expression of just exactly what and who we are.

Each of us has a particular way to express just exactly who and what she or he is. It is that "style" of energy use that makes working with different people and personalities interesting. The way in which each person deals with emotional responses is one of the indicators of an individual style. That style is yours alone and if you can discover how to use that style to the best advantage, you can release the energy of emotion in just the right way for you.

Others have different styles. The use of energy in action is very different with different people. One person may plan everything he or she does in great detail as a way to expend energy into action. Another person may act spontaneously and change directions frequently. Each person uses the energy of action to accomplish similar things, but in different ways. Neither way is wrong. But the attempt to make a spontaneous person become an organized and planned person can create a disaster. One client upon hearing that she was a "planned action" style took exception by saying that she used to be that way, but she had changed. She was very spontaneous now. As a matter of fact, she "can choose to be spontaneous anytime she wants." She realized almost immediately that she had in fact proven the style correct. She did plan her actions, even to be spontaneous!

We will talk more about energy styles as we go along but remember that these styles are not just physical or emotional, they are energy based. The emotional, physical, and mental energy we all use to solve problems, create new ideas, and achieve success can be seen in patterns. If you can recognize the ways in which you personally use your own energy, you can then make the most of your style to turn stress around into a positive factor in your life.

THE POWER OF ENERGY AS A POSITIVE FACTOR

Energy at any age is a wonder to behold. In her biography of the great Katherine Hepburn, Anne Edwards describes the triumphs and tragedies of this REMARKABLE WOMAN. "In 1984, a national survey elicited answers from forty-five hundred teenagers as to who they would name as their ten contemporary heroes." Katherine Hepburn's name appeared in the top seven choices with Michael Jackson, Clint Eastwood, and the Pope. (Edwards, page 331)

As a matter of fact, Ms. Edwards reports, "Kate was a notch above the Pope." Ms. Edwards explains that although many teenagers went to see the Academy award winning film ON GOLDEN POND to see Jane Fonda, the teenagers obviously were struck by the power of the lady Katherine. The image of "Katherine Hepburn, unafraid of age as of the icy waters of Squam Lake, her eyes brimming yet refusing to give into her deeply felt emotions when she knows her husband-lover-friend is about to die" (Edwards, page 331) made an impression on the teenage audience.

The effect of the emotional energy style of this lady upon her teenage and adult audiences was very much the same energy Marcel Vogel was talking about with us. The energy of balanced emotional release is a powerful force in changing our lives for the better.

"People are always blaming their circumstances
for what they are.
I don't believe in circumstances.
The people who get on in this world are the people
who get up and look
for the circumstances they want,
and if they can't find them,
make them."

George Bernard Shaw

THREE

THE POWER OF POSITIVE STRESS

Mark had arrived at the top of his corporate ladder. Step by step, he climbed the ladder of success until he was considered for a seat on the board of directors of his firm. Mark didn't want that seat on the board. To Mark, a seat on the board of directors would not give him the kind of stress he wanted. He thrived on his stress and requested another assignment. He wanted to be put in charge of one of the least productive districts in his firm's network of offices. Why? Why, when he had reached the pinnacle of his success and received accolades from his company and his peers, would he want to go to the bottom again? It was simple. *There was challenge at the bottom.*

Mark knew that he drew strength from challenges and stress. He had succeeded because those who were supposed to know the business kept telling him, "it couldn't be done." He had taken several unproductive districts and turned them into profitable successes, but he wanted to do more. He asked for the least desirable assignment because he knew without the stress of an "impossible" situation, he couldn't reach his personal best.

"What a man can be, he must be."

Abraham Maslow

25

STRESS AS AN OPPORTUNITY

Stress can be a extraordinary opportunity! Surprised? Can you imagine that stress can be anything other than a problem which must be handled, managed, or eliminated? All of the conventional wisdom says that stress is a lifestyle crisis for us. Stress is a disease to some and, certainly it is a stigma for many. The executive who admits to stress in his or her life might just as well announce incompetence. No one wants to admit that stress is a reality. But, isn't it interesting that stress is on everyone's lips these days?

As a matter of fact, there is an entire industry dedicated to help us manage our stresses. The "relaxation" industry thrives on people's pressure cooker lives. The spas, masseurs, and health clubs devoted to easing stress have proliferated in recent years until stress has become a fashionable affliction! *Stress is big business!* Pharmaceutical companies manufacture medications to help us with our stress. Musicians and music publishers produce relaxation tapes to help us soothe away our stress. Exercise gurus propose all types of programs to take all that energy of stress and burn it away.

With all of that, are we less stressed today than we were four years ago? 2 years ago? 50 years ago? Hardly! Workers' compensation claims naming stress as a major cause of a myriad of problems have risen in recent years to epidemic proportions. This is much to the dismay of health care insurance carriers, not to mention employers. Stress on the job is a major source of discussion among corporate leaders and human resource managers around the world. The stress levels of all those who work for a living in the 1990's seem to be escalating at alarming rates.

We all know this. We read the statistics. We know that we are all under fire from pressures of unbelievable intensities today. But, once again, there is the question. Why is stress something that the corporate and professional leader does not wish to acknowledge in his or her own life? What is the stigma attached to *it* that makes leaders wish not to have it attached to *them*? The stigma is in the definition of the word itself. What is stress?

When we look to the experts on stress, we often are told the same ideas over and over again. Stress is something about which many people have an opinion. Stress symptoms are often perceived as conditions to be eradicated or at least tamed so that you can continue with your life. In our research over the years, however, we have found that not all people view stress in that way. The high achievers of the business world very often thrive on stress and use it positively.

RECOGNIZING THE OPPORTUNITY FOR CHANGE

During one of our early seminars on stress, Mary Lee was teaching a relaxation visualization to the participants. In the 1980's these types of solutions to stress were very popular. She incorporated a "relaxation" image into her talk because the use of visualization has been used for years to combat stress. Using the mind to recall pleasant scenes is a tool for relaxation. So Mary Lee proceeded.

She asked the audience to sit back, close their eyes, and relax. As they sat there with their eyes closed, she described a scene to them of a calm pond on which they could place a raft and float out into the middle of the water. She guided them to climb onto the raft and float out into the middle of the pond and feel the support of the water under them. She went on to describe the gentle rocking of the raft as the water currents drifted under it.

Does this sound relaxing to you? Well, it did for most of the audience. Most, but not all. One unfortunate person in the audience could not swim and the idea of floating in the middle of a pond was terrifying. Forget that the pond was calm and the water gentle. Forget that the image was only imaginary and not real. Forget that the woman was safe in a hotel conference room miles away from any water. She was terrified. There was no relaxation here. Just more stress.

Mary Lee calmed the woman down and reassured her that she could make up any image she was comfortable with instead of the water. The idea was to relax the woman, not traumatize her. The entire episode led us to examine the reasons why the conventional stress/relaxation techniques worked for some and not for others.

Think Bite #2

Do you really believe that the imagination can be so powerful as to give people physical and emotional reactions like the one we just described? Well, try it yourself.

Sit back and relax. Try this exercise with your eyes closed. You will have to read it first, of course, then do it. With your eyes closed, imagine that you see a big, juicy, yellow lemon in front of you. Imagine what it smells like. Imagine the texture of the peel of the lemon. Turn it around in your mind and pick it up. Imagine that you are smelling it. Think about what a lemon smells like. Now, still with your eyes closed, cut into the lemon with a knife. Watch the juice ooze out of the lemon onto the countertop. Pick up one half of the lemon and take a bite of it. Imagine what it tastes like.

Now, close your eyes and do it. Don't have to, do you? You've probably already noticed saliva building up in your mouth just from *the thought of that juicy lemon*! Your thoughts can be very powerful. Not because you are anyone special, but just because the power of the mental images we can create are so tied into our whole system. If you want to, have someone read the passage above to you so that you can fully enjoy that lemon.

"Imagination is more important than knowledge."

Albert Einstein

RECOGNIZING THE STRESS SIGNALS

If we all dealt with our stresses in exactly the same way, there would be no room for the individual experiences which each of us has accumulated over years of living. Each person brings to these relaxation techniques his or her own special memories and experiences. Those memories trigger reactions which are different for everyone who uses these techniques. We are not all the same, so how can we treat our stress the same way?

Stress does cause symptoms which we all have witnessed or experienced. Some are severe and debilitating, but more often they are annoyances. To take this reality a step beyond the ordinary into the extraordinary, we need to look at the positive use of this stress. Some of the most powerful people we have met or have known through reputation use their stresses to succeed. Sometimes the success causes more stress and life becomes a challenge to maintain that success.

Donald Trump says in SURVIVING AT THE TOP, "I believe I've been helped by the realization that life is a series of struggles. And there's nothing I or anyone else can do about that. In fact, I've come to relish the struggles." (Trump, page 13)

On one point, we would disagree a bit with Mr. Trump. We believe that there is "something" that we can do about these series of struggles we all have. That "something" is turn the stress that comes from those struggles into positive action and achievement.

That "positive stress" is a recognition that the challenges of stress can be the opportunities and the possibilities for success. To many people, stress is and always will be a negative. But, wait, this mind of yours is capable of so much more than negative thinking. You can take stress and make it into an asset if you want.

Often we are reminded that when there are difficulties in early childhood or in adulthood that cause great and lasting trauma, the person is a victim to the trauma long after it has passed. We often hear from clients that they will never forget an event or situation which impacted on them in some way. That is true. They

29

never will forget because the memory of that event is always impressed upon the brain and its storage system. But the implication that the reactions to those events will always remain as they are we believe to be false. We have found that the traumatic events of the past, even though they are stored forever, can be altered.

Dr. Robert Ornstein in THE HEALING BRAIN considers society's view of stress from many perspectives. "Consider the current popular view of stress. People are seen as passive, helpless victims. Stressors of all sorts, from loss of a loved one to loss of our car keys, attack us, resulting in disease much as germs cause infections. The answer: avoid stress, change and challenge. Yet, stress does not result simply from exposure to events in the environment. The way we perceive and appraise an event, the availability and use of resources to cope the challenge, have more to do with the outcome than the raw event itself."(Ornstein, page 196)

We have dealt with cases of physical, sexual, and mental abuse. Some of the stories are devastating and often unspeakably compelling to us. Any case of abuse of whatever degree or type is destructive to the victim, but even that stress can be turned into a positive opportunity for those who understand that there is something that they can do. In the following chapters you will become familiar with many people whose stories illustrate one thing. Stress is an opportunity for change. Stress can lead to the achievement of personal power over adversity and emotional disability. There is a *positive stress factor.*

USING STRESS SIGNALS AS OPPORTUNITIES

Stress to many is defined as something which "gets us." How many times have you heard someone say, "The stress is killing me?" Or, "He's under a lot of stress these days?" Or, "I can't handle the stress anymore?" Stress sounds like it almost has a life all of its own. Stress is not an entity. "It" cannot reach out and grab you. Stress is not a caged animal to be "handled." Stress is not a disease which must be cured so that we can go on with our lives.

Miriam Stoppard, a well respected author, director of Syntex Pharmaceuticals, and hostess of her daily BBC magazine television program PEOPLE TODAY, recognizes the relationship between stress and energy. She believes that "as stress increases, efficiency initially increases but if the stress keeps going, the curve flattens out and efficiency drops steeply." Modifying behavior patterns makes "stress work for its living and transforms it into a source of energy." ($M_\&IT$, May, 1992, page 31)

It is this energy of stress which we can use positively. The energy we feel when we are challenged is the same energy we use for other purposes. Energy is a reality on many levels. We often hear people talk about increasing their "energy levels" to deal with some problem or other. "I just don't have any energy today," is a common phrase. When that energy level or that energy system is unbalanced for some reason, the result is what we all call "stress."

THE ENERGY SYSTEM

The energy system is the system of collected and connected physical, mental, and emotional parts of the individual. This energy system is connected by the "energy" which manages the system. The physical energy of the brain and nervous system, the chemical energy of the various chemical reactions, and the mental energy produced by the mind all combine into one system which we call the "energy system." It is through the energy system that all functions of the human system proceed.

We think and act and create. We eat and digest and eliminate. We walk and talk and sing. All of this we can do because of the energy system which takes everything we give it and transforms all of that material into different material for living. The substance of living is driven by the energy of the system. Without the communication within the system, there would be no living. Without the brain's communication pathways to the nervous system, you could not read these words. Without the mental energy of the mind, you could not comprehend these words. Without the physical energy to move, you could not take these words and use them.

The total energy system gives us the power to produce, create, live, and breathe every day. The energy system itself, like any other system, must be cared for and monitored to act efficiently. The system must be balanced just as your car must have the proper tire pressure, proper fuel, and proper maintenance to function. The human energy system must be balanced to function efficiently. Just as the government has checks and balances to assure proper functioning, the human system has many checks and balances on its own functioning. Without these abilities, the human energy system would be helpless. Let's think about it for a minute. Are you sitting down?

Comfortable? How do you know you are comfortable? How did you decide? Do you realize how complex that simple question and its answer are? In order to answer that question, a series of communication steps had to be taken. The first, most importantly, is the ability to actually read the question. You saw the words through the miracle of eyesight. You understood the words through the miracle of mental interpretation. You sent a message to another part of the brain to find the answer.

The second important step here is one of those intangible uses of energy we never think about consciously. The unconscious workings of the human brain to assess the rest of the physical body. In order to know if you are comfortable, the various elements of your physical, muscular, and skeletal system, as well as the organ systems, had to be checked. The brain literally asked a question in the same way a computer scans for information stored within it.

If you have stored material on a computer disk and then wish to print that material, the computer must first find out, through scanning, whether or not you have connected the printer to the computer, and if you have turned the printer's power source on! You may wish to print something, but if the computer checks and finds that it is physically impossible to do that, it will tell you.

Just so are the human brain and its communication pathways. The human brain checks to find out if it is possible to move and perform some function before it will execute that function. The human brain in this case checks to see if the muscles are stiff, sore, or in some other kind of discomfort. It checks to see if your stomach needs food or some other kind of attention. It checks to see if you need to empty your bladder or colon. After it has checked all of these systems through the complex nervous system, it then can "report" that everything seems to be comfortable.

After all of that communication and checking, that part of the brain informs the other parts and you have your answer. Voila! How simple!! Not really. You probably never think about the thousands of intricate maneuvers the human brain must perform for one simple task. Now, imagine what the mind has to do to create a sculpture, invent a complex computer mechanism, or to dream a dream.

Take a few minutes to think about what you just read. Think about the "miracle" that is you. You are a very complex system. Your energy system functions every minute of every day and never takes a vacation. From the first breath to the last, your system never shuts down. It works every day to make sure it, and you, survive. This is the prime directive which helps you to survive and thrive every day.

STRESS AND THE ENERGY SYSTEM

Now, what does all that have to do with stress? Remember that the system has a series of checks and balances built into itself to keep a close watch on your survival. Did you ever starve because you forgot to eat? Did you ever forget to take a breath because you were too busy? Did your heart ever "miss a beat" because your brain just got "sick and tired" of doing its job? Hardly.

The human energy system always knows what it is doing. Which is more than we can say usually about our conscious states! When something is wrong or off balance, the system, first, knows it, and then, tries to fix it. Usually it does that without your knowledge, but sometimes, it has to let you know what is going on. The system tells you everything. Sometimes, we just don't listen or understand the signals. Sometimes, we choose to ignore them. Sometimes, we can't ignore them.

Stress is the signal of an energy system which has a problem. It is out of balance and has to bring your attention to that fact. The stress does not come from outside your system. It is the system giving you a signal. Stress does not come out of nowhere and attack you when you least expect it. We cannot tell you how many times a client has said, "I felt this coming for a long time." The fact is that stress just doesn't happen. It comes along after the system has been placed in some position where there is an imbalance.

What do we mean by an "imbalance?" Think about the times you have said, "I have *too much* to do." Or, "I have *too little* time." Or, "This is just *too good* to be true." Yes, you can be unbalanced with something good as well as something bad. Remember the Holmes and Rahe stress scales we all took years ago that measured our stresses by numbering the events in our lives, such as marriage, death in the family, job demands, etc.? Sometimes, a very happy occasion can be very stressful. That doesn't mean that we are fooling ourselves when we are happy. We are not really just hiding our misery behind a mask. Happy times are very stressful because we are unbalanced. We really have swung to the opposite extreme of misery and we are once again unbalanced.

The result of this imbalanced situation, happy or not, is stress. Stress doesn't come from people or events, it comes from your reaction to those people or events. But, it isn't just the reaction to the people or events; it is your system's imbalance which causes that reaction we call stress. Stress affects different people in different ways. Some people thrive on stressful situations and really rise to the occasion while others are destroyed by stress, sometimes quite literally.

One of those who could have been destroyed by a stressful situation but was not is Warnaco's Linda Wachner. She is one of the highest paid female CEOs in the country, according to WORKING WOMAN magazine. In the next century, we may not refer to persons as male or female, but we still do live in a society which wants to designate gender, so we shall. Ms. Wachner is profiled in the May, 1992, issue of the magazine as the first woman in American corporate history to capture a company in a hostile takeover and then turn it successfully public. The story of Ms. Wachner's success is attributed to an experience when she was eleven years old. A chair was pulled out from under her and she spent two years immobilized in a body cast.

Ms. Wachner related the story to Ms. Maggie Mahar in the article. "My parents didn't know what to say or how to cope," she recalls. "It was a very hard thing to explain to a child, to get to the depths of a child's understanding. . . I was alone, with nothing to do except focus on tomorrow . . . Sometimes, when I'm very tired, I still dream about that silver traction triangle hanging over my head." Ms. Wachner grew up with a purpose in life. "During that lonely childhood," Ms. Mahar reports, "she stored up energy like a solar battery storing sunlight." (Mahar, WORKING WOMAN, May, 1992, pages 105)

Ms. Wachner's story is like many stories we have heard over the years from achievers and leaders in business and the professions who are pushed toward a goal or pressured into success by sheer determination. Ms. Mahar goes on to say that "Linda Wachner succeeded not because she wanted to, not because she hoped to, but because she felt she had to."

"Strong lives are motivated by dynamic purposes."

Kenneth Hildebrand

"CHALLENGE" IS ANOTHER WORD FOR STRESS

The best philosopher in the world is named "Anonymous." There is even a statue in his/her honor in Budapest near the park in the center of the city where he/she sits silent and hooded in a place of honor. Anonymous said many wonderful things over the centuries. He/She is quoted in all languages and in all countries. The wisdom of one quote certainly applies to the subject of the positive use of stress. "A diamond is a chunk of coal that made good under pressure."

Frederick Harmon, the author of THE EXECUTIVE ODYSSEY, discusses the stresses of the executive who succeeds by unleashing the power behind those stresses. "The higher the aspiration . . . the greater the energy released . . . the greater the achievement, the greater the power to propel the individual forward in life." (Harmon, page 41) Stress can propel us forward if we use the energy of that stress to find our own power to make changes and to eventually triumph over what could be a disaster.

There is no greater stress than the stress of devastating illness. Illness rearranges our lives and sometimes can be the most positive stress to propel us into some new realization about our lives. Stress-related symptoms and conditions account for many modern maladies. Some of the recent literature of the medical sciences community has attributed over 80 percent of humankind's problems physically and mentally to stress. If not identified as "stress" at least, it is identified as a "lifestyle problem." Unhealthy lifestyles cause a vast number of physical and mental dysfunctions and the list is growing every day.

Remember though, the title of this book is THE POSITIVE STRESS FACTOR. We believe that stress is a signal and nothing more dire than that. Stress is a signal or sign that the system is unbalanced and must be helped in some way. Stress is the challenge which can cause us to change our course. Perhaps, relaxation is the answer. Perhaps, delegating responsibility more effectively is the answer. There are many reasons for the signal and there may be

36

many alternative solutions. The important thing is that you address the signal when you feel it.

Think Bite #3

Now, let's think about your own body. When you feel stressed, where do you feel it physically? Come on, you have had some experience with stress, right? Where did you feel it? Did you ever have a headache from too much stress? Did it feel like a pressure over your eyes? Across your forehead?

Did you ever find it hard to breathe because it felt like someone was standing on your chest? Did you ever have knots in your stomach when you were facing some stressful situation?

Did your lower back ever ache when you were working on a deadline?

Take a minute to think about those "stress points" on your body right now. We'll tell you where they are. You can check the ones you have had. The first one is at the top of your head. You know the feeling that your "top is going to blow off?"

The second one is the forehead. The third is the throat. Remember when you couldn't talk because your throat was dry and tight? The fourth stress point is a favorite for stressed people---the chest and heart. The old "solar plexus" is the fifth stress point. This is where those ulcers grow! The last two points are on your backside. One at your waistline over your spine and one at the tip of your tailbone.

How many of these do you remember feeling? Count them. Do you remember when you felt them? Take some time to think about them. Maybe you'll want to do what some of the clients do. Keep a journal of the places on your body that you feel stress. If you keep a journal, you will notice patterns to your stress. When you see the pattern, then you are ready to use that stress pattern to make changes. But, right now, just make a note of those points which seem to bother you from time to time.

TURNING STRESS INTO AN ASSET

If we become aware of stress as a positive asset in life, then recognizing the signal takes on a whole new meaning for us. To understand "positive stress" we must explain the beginning of Energy Dynamics^R. The beginning was with a young woman named Jo who was searching for the reasons for her own ill health. Jo was a young doctor learning a great deal about her own profession and what that healing art could do for her patients and for herself, but it was not enough. She herself was ill and becoming more so. During a convention, Jo became so ill that she literally collapsed at the feet of her old mentor and teacher, Dr. Benedict.

Dr. Benedict helped Jo through that difficult day and she survived the rest of the convention. The doctor had used a technique unfamiliar to Jo and Jo was not only grateful, but intrigued. But she didn't have the time or inclination to learn more during those days.

She went back to her work and almost forgot the incident. Fortunately, Jo's body would not let her forget. A few days passed and she became desperately ill. She was dizzy. Her blood pressure plummeted to dangerously low levels. She experienced a debilitating headache through her work day. She was almost nonfunctioning.

At this point, Dr. Benedict called to invite Jo to a seminar. It was being taught by a man who had taught Dr. Benedict some of the material she had used to help Jo at the convention. Reluctantly, Jo went. She felt so bad physically that she would rather have stayed home, but something drove her to attend this seminar. While she was there, Jo suffered a great deal. Sitting still was almost impossible and she was truly not learning anything. She was caught in a fog of vague pains and discomfort. The stress symptoms she experienced made her irritable and argumentative. The seminar leader tried to talk with Jo and encourage her to pay attention to the signals her body was giving her, but she was stubborn. She came up with a thousand reasons for her aches and pains. She was overworked. She was hungry. She was bored.

Jo resisted every suggestion to give her body more attention. She was like many health care professionals who think that care is for their patients and not for themselves. Many of us warn our clients and patients to slow down, eat properly, and pay attention to warning signs, but do we take our own advice? Sadly, not very often. When we collapse, we pay attention.

Jo was racing down the road to her next collapse and she didn't see it coming. It happened one day in her clinic. She was working with a patient and found that she could not stand for more than a few minutes without resting. As the patient talked, Jo found herself not hearing the words clearly. She was drifting in a sea of detachment. She knew what she was doing, but it was mechanical. Jo had lost the connection with her own world. She left the clinic exhausted and completely detached.

Jo called another doctor and asked for his advice. She knew she could not continue this way, but really didn't know what to do. With all of her training, she still wanted a quick fix to get her through the days. He told her to take time off, rest, and stop pushing. Well, he was history. *Jo didn't have time to rest, take time off, and stop pushing.* There were *patients to see, people to help, and places to go!* She resented her body for letting her down. All of her life, she had been able to push through and win by sheer force of will. *Until now.* Her will was being blocked.

It was here that Jo faced her next collapse. She fell down a flight of stairs rushing to her next appointment. She could not move. She was finally faced with a situation she could not ignore. Jo found herself staring at her own x-rays and seeing the results of her own illness. Jo was looking at the very first signs of deterioration in the skeletal system. The doctor asked her "What are you going to do about this?"

It seemed to her a rather odd question. She searched his eyes for some further information about what her answer should be, but there was no answer in his eyes. The answer was in her mind. She hesitated for a few seconds and said, "I'm going to get rid of it."

This story sounds fairly conventional in these days of alternative therapies for every disease known to humankind; but, the story does not stop there. The story is not being told because of the victory over a disease. What is important here is that Jo decided to take charge of her life and do what her body and mind together could accomplish if they knew how.

Her energy level was definitely at its lowest, but there was something about the stress which caused Jo to take positive steps to overcome what could have been a disaster. She started slowly and steadily to reassess her life and lifestyle. Jo turned her stress into an asset to find a new goal in life. She searched for a new meaning in her life. *She started to change her life.*

Jo's story can be told in some form by hundreds or thousands of people who have faced some stress in their lives and who have overcome it. Norman Cousins spent a great deal of his later life inspiring others to fight back and to survive great challenges. Franklin Delano Roosevelt faced paralysis during the prime of his life and went on to lead an entire nation through some of the blackest days of the 20th century. Helen Keller searched for a light instead of "cursing the darkness." Chief Joseph of the Nez Perce Indians, like so many of his Native American brothers and sisters, faced challenges in his own land to triumph over injustices.

Oliver Wendell Holmes believed that "what lies behind us and what lies before us are tiny matters compared to what lies within us." What lies within us we never suspect until there is stress. This stress not only helps us to make decisions about personal challenges, but also professional ones. This stress we talk in our careers can be turned into power if we turn the stress into an asset for achievement.

"Do or Do Not.
There is no "try."

Yoda in *The Return of the Jedi*

THE DYNAMICS OF CHANGE

Stress is an opportunity. It can only become an opportunity when you look at stress as a dynamic for change. Stress can be used to understand the problems you face and it can help solve them. Stress is very powerful when used negatively, but it can be equally powerful when used positively. Stress is a factor in pushing us into achievement. Bert Decker, in his book, YOU'VE GOT TO BE BELIEVED TO BE HEARD, talks about the "First Brain" theory. Decker has taught literally thousands of executives and professionals over the years to use the First Brain in communication. The First Brain, according to Decker, is the most basic part of the brain. "It is real, it is physical and it is powerful; the seat of the emotions." (Decker, book jacket blurb, front)

In order to control and use this First Brain in our communication, Decker says that there is a "dynamic tension" which comes from the pressure and stress to perform. It is this "dynamic tension" which Decker says gives great performers the edge. "It's the pressure aspect of public speaking and athletic performance . . . athletes direct the pressure and tension they feel into the energy needed to power their performance." (Decker, page 168)

It is this "dynamic tension" which we call "the positive stress factor." The positive stress factor can teach those who are already achievers in some way to take the stress, pressure, and tension of everyday situations and use that stress as a positive factor for change and success.

LEADERSHIP AND CHANGE

Stress is a challenge without which leaders cannot succeed. The best thing about failure in business is that it causes stress. A leader achiever takes that failure and learns from it. The stress of losing a contract, losing a chance, or losing a partner forces a leader to act in some way. One very close friend of ours said once, "I don't want to eliminate my stress. I need the stress to motivate me." He was right.

As a matter of fact, let's get back to the physical body for a minute. Can you imagine what your physical condition would be without the tension of the muscles to hold you up? Without that tension in the system, you would look a bit like a jellyfish. You would have no form and would look like a blob of flesh with no shape. Without tension in your arms you could not hold this book. Without the vascular tension in your blood vessels, there would be no blood pressure. Eventually, and not too long, you would not exist without blood pressure. It is the tension of the physical body that keeps you standing and walking.

Remember a time when your arms and legs felt like noodles because you were ill? Without the stress in the legs and arms, you could not function. The wonderful thing about stress is that it is both positive and negative. The dynamic struggle of tension and relaxation gives us energy and it is that energy which provides the power to move our bodies. The stress provides the dynamic motion of the energy system.

Dynamic is defined as "marked by continuous change." If your system were not dynamic, there would be no change. If there were no change, you would never have grown from zygote to fetus to baby to teenager to adult. The dynamic changes in the energy system made you what you are today. The stress you feel from time to time and the stresses you don't feel keep you going. From all of that stress, energy, and dynamic change comes power. *That power is and can be positive.*

The positive factor in our lives is an extraordinary opportunity to change, to learn, and to use the stress of our system to move forward. Stress can compel us forward to achieve more than we can dream and, some of what we do dream. It is not easy. It is not magic. It is not impossible. The "impossible" is not unattainable, it just hasn't been done yet.

As we learn about stress and its positive effect on your life, remember stress uncontrolled and ignored can have a disastrous effect on you. The point of THE POSITIVE STRESS FACTOR is not just that stress can be positive, but that you must learn to listen to the your own system's signals and then do something positive with those signals. The power of positive thinking does not work if you sit in the middle of a freeway, thinking that you will not die before you are 105 years old. If you want to think positively, that's all well and good, but you must also recognize that you have to do something to support that thought. You have to move from the danger. Get off the freeway! You can't ignore the signals. You must move! Will Rogers had a twist on this same subject when he said, "Even if you are on the right track, you'll get run over if you just sit there."

Stress is a great subject for a leader to explore because as a leader, you already know about stress. You use it every day. *Are you using it as positively as you might?* Do you want to unlock more and more of the dynamic energy within you to achieve even more than you dreamed possible? Mark, the achiever you met at the beginning of this chapter is a good friend and once inscribed his stationery with the following: "Too low they build who build beneath the stars." Needless to say, he is a leader. He is a powerhouse of dynamic changes and achievement. He took his small business and created a multi-million dollar dynasty. The stars were calling and he decided to build his life by reaching for the highest platform he could find.

A great deal of stress goes into building for the stars. You may fall at any moment. Who wants to be looking up toward something all the time? Take a chance and enjoy the view from the top. Build on your stress for power and turn that stress into the biggest asset you have.

"If the doors of perception were cleansed, man would see things as they are, infinite."

William Blake

FOUR

THE POWER OF ENERGY DYNAMICS^R

Energy Dynamics^R is an approach to stress unparalleled in its effectiveness. There are those who have used this program successfully over the years to change their lives dramatically. But, in order to do that, each person had to have an inexplicable something we call a "self-core." This element is the ability to risk change. *It is not enough to want change, you must be willing to risk that change.* James M. Kouzes and Barry Z. Posner in THE LEADERSHIP CHALLENGE talk about change and how *leaders* "are pioneers--people who are willing to step out into the unknown. They are people who are willing to take risks." (Kouzes and Posner, page 8).

All of those who have used Energy Dynamics^R in the past years have taken the same information found in THE POSITIVE STRESS FACTOR and used that information in their professional and personal lives. They were leaders who wanted more out of life than just survival. One of our good friends summed up her philosophy of "positive stress" with a story about her decision at 17 years of age to become a nurse. Many young women of that age in the 1950's wanted to become nurses, but, there was a difference with our friend. She was a young African-American woman who attended a Catholic school and, as she said, was definitely a "minority."

44

In those days, a young woman of color could not be taken seriously if she wanted to be a nurse and attend an all white school. She told us how she confronted the Mother Superior. The Mother Superior was kind, but carefully explained that there would be a problem with our friend attending the segregated school because the parents of the other girls would take exception to a "Negro" as a roommate. Remember, it was the 1950's. Before Dr. King. Before the Civil Rights Law. Before all that. This 17 year old girl had only herself and her own dream to stand on.

The Mother Superior explained that if our friend would "pass as Mexican," they might be able to satisfy the objections of the parents. Our friend told us that she sat for a few seconds, thinking about those words, and then replied, "Well, I don't know. You see, for 17 years my parents have raised a Negro daughter. They would be so shocked to find out that I was Mexican after all these years." *That is a self-core.* That is a person who has that intangible something to risk. *That is a leader.* She has gone on to become an even stronger leader as a successful university administrator and speaker. Oh, by the way, she also did become a nurse and is still African-American. She likes to tell that story because it means that she redirected the energy of negativity into a positive through the use of that inner self-core which gives us all the possibility to be whatever we want.

Energy Dynamics[R] is a program which builds on that self-core to use stress and energy in a positive way. This program explores the possibility that each person is not merely a collection of unconnected thoughts, reflexes, and experiences. Each individual is actually a unified system of body functions, mental complexities, and personal values which have become so enmeshed within the person that these parts cannot be separated from each other. Each system which we call an "energy system" contains information which has been collected, learned, and altered through the minutes, seconds, and micro-seconds we live.

THE RISK OF CHANGE

Sometimes the risk to change this energy system is too great and the challenge is too traumatic. Ted was a young man who had always done what others expected of him. He was terribly unhappy with both his personal and his professional life. As a matter of fact, Ted didn't really know how he had chosen his profession. He just seemed to wake up one day and found himself working for a company as its director of sales. He had not consciously chosen this life, but there he was. When we first met Ted, he was suffering from all of the common stress symptoms. He had insomnia. He was gaining weight uncontrollably. He was withdrawn around his friends. He was searching for someone to make it "all better."

When Ted was given the opportunity to make changes about his life, he was, at first, excited at the prospect. But, Ted's energy system had been taught over the years that he was not capable of making any sound decisions. His system had collected information which made it impossible for him to risk without a guarantee. As a result, Ted remained as he was. He listened, but did not hear. He took in all of the information, but did not process it. He did not act.

Ted was one of those people we call "the tumbleweed people." "Tumbleweed people" are those who are battered around by the winds of circumstance, drifting wherever the wind blows them, without trying to direct their own lives. We'll come back to them later. Ted knew on some level that he was in trouble, and he knew that he had to change something. He just didn't have any experience making up his own mind. Ted was trapped by the wishes and desires of other people in his life. Even though his physical body and his emotions were trying to get him to make changes, Ted did not have the internal drive to risk any changes.

This human energy system has the ability to collect, to store, and eventually, to retrieve all the pieces of information stored within it in a matter of seconds. The part of this system with which we are all most familiar is the physical body which appears to run "by itself" most of the time. We don't stop to think if our hearts are beating properly, unless there is an irregularity. Then, we are frightened! Normally, we hardly notice the beating of the heart, the blinking of the eyes, or the breathing of the lungs. We certainly never notice the blood flowing, the food digesting, or the brain remembering details! If you do, you are rare indeed. OR, you have had a problem with one of those functions which has made you hypersensitive to it. It's funny how only when we are in trouble do we notice the "unnoticeable."

Over the years, we realized that those who were forced to *notice the unnoticeable* were often those who had risked change. Maybe that was because there are no alternatives. Or, maybe it is because that "self-core" we mentioned earlier causes the individual to *want to change.* Ted did not make the changes he needed to make because he had never developed that "self-core" which would allow him to make his own decisions. There are some who have developed that ability.

THE CHALLENGE OF CHANGE

Carol is a brilliant research scientist who has been bombarded by physical maladies all her life. She has truly done it all and tried it all! Her life was one long series of doctors and hospitals and pills and pain. Eventually, her mental and emotional state became so bad that she became what some call a victim of "Chronic Pain Syndrome." Her energy system had become so full of mental and physical impressions that it could no longer function as it was. She needed help, but she resisted asking for any. She had seen too many doctors over too many years. *She wanted no more.*

Carol is well-read and accomplished in her field. She has a keen scientist's mind for detail and proof. Initially, the concepts of Energy Dynamics^R were suspect to her. She questioned every nuance and challenged every recommendation. She has a mind of her own and certainly makes you know that. She was desperate for help, just as Ted had been, but there was a vital difference. *Carol knew Carol.*

Carol made her own decisions. She wanted control of her life and she needed the tools to find that control.

One very good friend once said, "I never want to be in a position where I "need" something or someone. I always want to "want" and make the choice to have." Carol was the epitome of that concept. She made choices based on her own system's judgment, not the judgment of other people.

As time went on, Carol took all that she had been told about Energy Dynamics^R, rearranged it, analyzed it, and then, made her own decisions. She chose to risk a change. Today, Carol has accomplished more than she expected. Her professional life is satisfying because it is full of possibilities. Her personal life is just that. *Personal.* She lives each day as she chooses. The important thing is that she no longer needs anyone to teach her. She has learned her own truth and uses that truth in her own way. This is the empowerment which comes from having a "self-core" and the ability to move beyond stress into a positive and dynamic life. Carol's physical body was the source of her challenge in stress, but *facing its challenge was the key to her power.*

THE PHYSICAL REALITY OF ENERGY

The physical body is only one part of a greater system which constantly communicates with the process we call "conscious thinking." The thoughts we have begin somewhere and go somewhere. Usually! The thinking process is one which scientists have explored, studied, and tested until we hardly know what to think anymore! The functioning of the brain and mind are to many of us a complex series of mysterious surprises. We think . . . therefore, we are. But what are we? Why do we think? We will leave those questions for the scientists to explore and explain. One of the most accomplished research scientists we have known was Marcel Vogel, a senior scientist for IBM for 27 years. You met Marcel in the last chapter.

His exploration of the brain and the mind forms the basis of much of the work described in THE POSITIVE STRESS FACTOR.

We met and spoke with Marcel many times over the years. His theories of energy helped to push us into more research. All of the scientists who have come before us have given such a legacy upon which to build practical tools with which to apply their work. The theories of every scientist, whether proven or unproven, are never lost. Every step along the way leads to another step and a new discovery. For all of those steps we are all indebted, but, the practical application of science often escapes us.

We have watched many researchers and teachers over the years spend years studying the effects of everything from food, to thoughts, to environments, to exercise. Most of these studies have served one purpose. That purpose is to point out that there is some problem. . . that there is a relationship among the factors they study.

We sat through a seminar one weekend on the subject of stress. The outline of the seminar contained 10 modules of sessions. Nine of those sessions dealt with the identification of what causes stress. One session dealt with possible solutions! We already knew we were stressed, *but what could we do about it?!*

It was this frustration which led us to explore the energy system. *There just had to be something more to the system than a mass of unconnected thought patterns and reflexes.* If we could understand how the total system worked, then we could teach other people to use that system more effectively.

Our goal in Energy Dynamics^R was to discover how the physical body and the emotions worked hand in hand to create stress. The system works well most of the time because there is "the prime directive" at work. This directive explained how the system communicated within itself to use energy efficiently.

Our concept of the brain and the mind is that these two parts of the energy system are actually separate functions and not the same. The brain is part of the physical body and as such works as the computer for the rest of the functioning system of physical responses and needs. The brain commands the rest of the physical system day by day and second by second to carry on the necessary functions of the system itself. In this way the brain is the control mechanism for the so-called unconscious functions of the physical body. The brain must continue to function until the death of the physical body. The brain is literally the "last to go." Without the brain, there is no physical functioning.

The mind, on the other hand, in our description of the energy system, is that part of the system which *interprets* the events, experiences, and relationships we establish as we live each day. It is the mind which gives meaning to the words we learn. It is the mind which interprets our actions and those of others. It is the mind to which we go when we want to remember something and to alter those memories.

The mind is the key to the memory and it is this key that we can use to change, not the experience of memory, but the interpretation of memory. This is the theory of Energy Dynamics[R.] The mind can reveal experience from memory so that the person can learn from that experience and alter the attached emotional responses connected to the experience. More about this later.

CHOOSING TO CHANGE

One of the failures we experienced in our work was with a woman named Catherine. Catherine was the director of nursing at a large city hospital. All of her life had been centered around medicine and hospitals. She prided herself on her knowledge of the human body. She knew the seriousness of pain and suffering, and she felt dedicated to helping others be relieved of their pain. All of her education had pivoted upon the fact that this was a serious business, this business of disease and healing.

Catherine came to one of our seminars and listened very carefully, observing others in the room who had been to other training sessions of ours in the past. She watched with some rather detached expressions on her face until finally, she approached us during a break. She said, "*Don't you people realize that the subject of stress is very serious?* I can't believe that you can find anything funny about it. These other people can't possibly be here because they have any stress in their lives. *Look at them.* They are laughing and carrying on. I just can't believe you are not going to teach us anything. After all, I have paid my tuition and *I wanted to learn something today.*"

Catherine was very upset that we had taken what she considered a very serious subject so lightly. Her memory banks were full of images of pain, suffering, and distress. Her energy system was so impacted with negative thoughts about stress that the possibility of anything positive connected to stress was beyond her understanding. Catherine went on her way. As she walked away, we both thought how sad it was that she had wanted to learn something, and did not. She wanted to learn something, but *she wanted that "something" to match what she already knew to be true.* She didn't want to have any of her ideas challenged.

Not all of us reach the same crossroads at the same time. We all gain new knowledge when it is necessary. That leads us into the last part of the energy system. This part we call the "personal values" aspect.

THE EMOTIONAL REALITY OF ENERGY

This last part of the energy system in Energy Dynamics[R] is the seat of those intangible values and those personal attitudes about the larger questions of life. These intangibles include the person's relationship with the world in general, his or her attitude toward death, his or her belief in the unproven, and finally, the person's individual preferences and styles of living. This part of the system is, of course, the most difficult to explain or to explore, for that matter. But we do explore it in Energy Dynamics[R].

Because this "personal values" part is so intangible and based on a person's individual view of the world and himself or herself, this is the part which many times gives all of us trouble. It is also that part with which the mind must grapple from time to time when new experiences enter into our lives. The new experiences require a redefinition of life and the meaning of life.

Patricia had been climbing her own corporate ladder for many years and had succeeded where many before her had failed. One of her good friends told her at one time that the most stressful thing about business is that you may find someday that when you reach the top of the corporate ladder, you could discover that your ladder has been leaning against the wrong wall.

Patricia's career had been developing rather well but one day she discovered that her ladder was leaning against the wrong wall. She worked very hard to get where she was. She had sacrificed family and friends to the cause of corporate success. The "glass ceiling" had shattered above her and she found herself sitting at the top of the mountain. She was indeed a successful woman. She was a successful person.

Patricia's world fell apart one warm summer day when her husband announced that he was leaving. Not just for the day. But for life. He had found someone he loved and he wanted to develop that new relationship. He loved Patricia and he loved their children, but he had discovered that his long hidden sexual preference could not stay hidden any longer.

Needless to say, Patricia tottered off her ladder of success. Her world had changed in an instant and she had some serious redefinitions to accomplish if she was to survive. Patricia reacted as most would in her situation. She was angry. She was shocked. She was helpless. She could not change the situation; she had to readjust in some way. Patricia had always felt that she had a handle on her emotional and mental view of the world as a whole. She felt she was a liberated woman who had a high sense of acceptance for other lifestyles, other ethnic groups, and other people's creeds.

All of that acceptance came to her in one crashing moment of her life. She had stood behind her principles and beliefs, now it was time to live them. Patricia moved on with her life by defining her feelings about her new situation. She returned to her work, and she supported both her husband and her children in the difficult weeks and months ahead. Patricia was backed up to the stressful wall and she had to act. What made her different from others in the same situation? The difference we believe is that Patricia had a "self-core" which allowed her to gather herself together and redefine her personal values system.

The changes in her life were dramatic, but the changes we all face are dramatic in some way. As we go along day by day, we are all faced with redefinitions and challenges to the personal values we all have. It is the stress of those challenges which can be used positively to readjust our lives so that those challenges do not destroy us.

Discovering that your ladder is leaning against the wrong building is not the tragedy it may seem. You can move the ladder if it is necessary. Or, you can start climbing a different ladder.

THE BALANCED REALITY OF THE ENERGY SYSTEM

We are complex systems of reflexes, both natural and learned. We are complex systems of experiences, both pleasant and unpleasant. We are also complex systems of values, both imposed upon us and self-imposed. The Energy Dynamics[R] approach is that these complex systems, whether tangible or intangible, can be explored if there is one common thread weaving itself throughout the complexity.

That common thread is the energy. This same energy is what Virginia Satir, a pioneer in family therapy and internationally acclaimed group leader and therapist, describes in THE NEW PEOPLEMAKING. Satir explains that in order to find a balance in our lives, we must imagine "that inside each of us is a power center responsible for maintaining life . . . Each center has a generator that produces energy to continue life." (Satir, page 30). It is this energy which initiates and guides behavior, according to Satir.

Finding that balance in our lives can sometimes be an exhausting search, but if we can use the energy of our systems to find that balance, there can be great rewards. The power of the balance comes from the conscious control of the system.

Think Bite #4

One of the best examples of balance we have seen is in the movie THE KARATE KID. Pat Morita as the wise teacher demonstrates balance to his young student by giving him several tasks to do around the teacher's house. The first task involves washing cars. But the technique is special because the old man tells the student to apply the soap with one hand and rinse with the other. Apply wax with one hand and buff with the other. He demonstrates painting by stroking up and down slowly and methodically. As the young man progresses with his work, he is learning a valuable lesson about balance and timing. This will serve him well with the karate lessons to come, but the importance of the balance is that he is being taught control and discipline.

The young man learns a great deal from his lesson in balance, and you are about to learn one, too. Think about breathing again. As you breathe in imagine that you are preparing yourself to do some major task. Remember lifting heavy pieces of furniture? As you prepare to lift, what do you do? You take a deep breath. When you were about to have your first job interview, what did you do before you spoke? You took a deep breath. When you perhaps asked for your first date, you took a deep breath. The inhalation is a preparation. A way to signal your system that something is about to happen for which you need some energy.

When you pause after the inhalation, hold your breath for a short time. Remember when you lifted that heavy sofa? You held your breath for a second or two. When you answered the questions on your job interview, you held your breath before answering. When you asked for that date, you held your breath before saying the words. The pause is like a gathering of energy or gathering of power to do something.

Now, you exhale. When did you exhale as you were moving furniture? After you set the piece down, right? When you were finished with the questions in your job interview, you sighed, right? When the object of your affection accepted your date, you breathed easier. When something is accomplished, we exhale.

Try an experiment. Breathe in deeply and hold your breath for a few seconds. As you hold your breath, what do you notice happening to you? Do you feel tension the longer you hold the pause? Experiment with holding your breath longer and longer. Be careful that you don't make yourself dizzy. But, try to hold the breath and observe what you feel. As you hold the breath the "power" of that breath seems to grow. The power comes from the tension which might be called "dynamic tension" as Decker calls it. In other words, the tension or stress of the pause causes you to sense a certain kind of power in the breathing process you probably never noticed before.

Now, as you breathe out, think about that part of the cycle as the accomplishment part. Think about the exchange of the oxygen and carbon dioxide that just happened. Think about the release of tension and the relaxation of the lungs as you exhale your breath. It's a little like isotonic or isometric exercise. The benefit from the exercise comes from the tension in the muscle building and then releasing. This action of tension and release tones the muscle fiber and strengthens the muscle for the next contraction.

As you breathe in and out slowly over the next few minutes, think about the cycle and the tension which you feel while you hold your breath. Notice something about the exhaled breath and the relaxation you feel. We'll do some exercises with breath later on, so practice breathing until we get there.

THE TUMBLEWEED PEOPLE

"Energy" in Energy Dynamics[R] involves not only emotional energy, but also physical energy in a package which together comprise the energy system. This system is the base from which the self-core can direct its own power to succeed and accomplish whatever you want. The common thread of energy is both a physical and an emotional reality.

This energy is the source of the communication between the brain and physical body which uses electrical impulses and chemical energy within the nervous system to carry out directives in the physical body. This energy is also the power of the memory storage unit of the brain which collects experiences and preserves them for future reference. The brain without energy could not carry out this important function. It is this function which allows us to live our lives without thinking about the countless minute activities which go on day after day without our conscious control or attention. Without some "energy," we cannot think clearly. Without "energy," we cannot move. Without "energy," we cannot live.

This energy is a powerful source to understand the ways in which we can monitor our own lives and learn from experience. We like to use the analogy of the "tumbleweed" to explain. The tumbleweed moves around its world without really resting in any one place. The tumbleweed is blown from place to place by the winds of change and does not appear to control very much of its life on this earth.

People sometimes move about their world like the tumbleweeds. They move here or there not by their own conscious choices, but because of the winds of change which blow them sometimes completely off their course into new territory. The tumbleweed does not control its destiny. Some people don't either. Some people, as Mama Rose in GYPSY sings, "live their life in a living room." There is little which moves them to conscious action. There is little which challenges them to act in any way that is decisive. The tumbleweed people survive life. They do not "live" it. The

56

tumbleweed people talk about "luck" and "chance." These people never risk anything.

The tumbleweed people do not create their own opportunities. The tumbleweed people take a precious gift of life and use it up day by day. Sometimes they are surprised at the end of that life that they have not accomplished anything.

If you are reading this book, you are not a tumbleweed. If you are reading this book, you are already connected to your conscious decision making processes and are exploring new information. The secret to a "non-tumbleweed" life is to explore new ideas all the time. You may reject those new ideas, but at least, you have made that conscious decision yourself.

THE *POSSIBILITIES* OF ENERGY DYNAMICS[R]

We have a very good friend who decided about three years ago to find out more about herself and her world. She wanted to find out what she had missed in her life and to find new horizons to explore. She took course after course offered, read book after book, and traveled to as many new places as she could find. She was very excited with her new discoveries and she shared these with us from time to time. She picked up new ideas and tried them on like new coats. She added to her base of knowledge and she reveled in her discoveries. At one point she worried that in order to explore the new she had to give up on the old.

She felt that life had a finite number of possibilities and that if she chose one thing instead of another, she was being disloyal to the one she replaced. It took a long time before she learned by herself that each of us is the compilation of everything we discover and everyone we know. Life is like a giant quilt to which pieces are added over the years to give brilliance to the pattern. The quilt does not have to be redesigned every time we add something to it. We only add new dimensions to our lives with every experience.

Our friend is a joy to watch as she explores the new and the undiscovered. She is becoming a magical combination of thoughts and ideas that she adds to her life. We should not be threatened by those who change, nor should be threats ourselves to those around us. Changes and risks make life exciting and dynamic. We must take the risks from time to time or become stagnant.

Barbra Streisand once remarked, "I can say, 'I am terribly frightened and fear is terrible and awful and it makes me uncomfortable.' Or I could say 'Get used to being uncomfortable. It is uncomfortable doing something that's risky.' But so what? Do you want to stagnate and just be comfortable.?"

We do not want you to accept everything you read in this book without questioning it. We do not pretend to know everything there is to know about any of the subjects here. But, we do intend to give you some food for thought about a subject we have explored for many years. The ideas here are just that . . . ideas. These are ideas, however, which do not come from some magical crystal ball or from some dream one of us dreamed many years ago. These ideas have been the result of years of listening to the problems, frustrations, fears, and thoughts of our many clients and friends.

Most of these people are people like you who have lived lives of achievement. Their lives have been filled with both negative and positive experiences. They have stored the memories of those experiences for years and years until, at some point in their lives, they needed to learn from those experiences. The approach of Energy Dynamics^R has been to teach these achievers to learn from their experiences and to use their own systems to change their perceptions of their experiences.

The stories you read here are about real people exploring real fears, anger, and, in some cases, real joy. One important aspect of Energy Dynamics^R is that "negative" and "positive" are two sides of the same coin. Negative experiences are neither to be ignored nor looked upon with fear. Negative experiences do not exist. *Negative reactions to experiences do exist!* It is not the *experience* which is negative. It is *what we do with the experience* which can be either negative or positive. A negative reaction is one in which nothing is learned. A positive reaction is one in which something is learned. Any experience teaches us something. It is up to us to consciously decide whether we will learn from the experience or not.

The stories you read here are stories about people learning and changing. There are stories about people exploring fearful parts of themselves and coming out on the other side of the exploration with understanding. Some of the stories are simple. There is the story of a woman who was hurt in an automobile accident. In the same accident, her mother was also hurt badly. Neither woman was permanently injured by the collision, but the fear of such a permanent result caused the younger woman to be afraid of the possibility of another accident. She was paralyzed by the fear and had all of the symptoms of anxiety, such as sweating palms and rapid heartbeat, when she even thought about getting into a car again.

Now, you can easily understand the source of her fear and the reaction she had to such a horrible accident. You can understand why she would be fearful of a recurrence. Well, guess what? She could, too, on a conscious level. But, why was she still struggling every time she faced a similar situation? She struggled because although the experience was consciously understood, unconsciously her emotional, intangible reactions were all intact in her memory. Without exploring the energy of the experience and the energy of her reactions to it, she was tied to the emotions.

So, what did she do? She learned to explore the experience not consciously, but rather through her energy system storage. She recalled the memory and explored why she reacted in such a way to the danger. She did not do this exploration through hypnosis or conventional psychoanalysis. Nor did she do this through any magical means. She simply learned to recall the memory of the event, look at that one event from her new perspective, not the old one of memory, and change her perception of the emotional reaction to it.

MEMORY PICTURES OF YOUR LIFE

Imagine that your memory banks are being filled with approximately 27 "pictures" per second. That means that every 27th of a second your mind makes a mental "picture" or record of an event. Imagine every second of every minute of every hour of every day of every week of every month of every year of your life, millions, billions, and trillions of "pictures" are stored. And you don't even need a memory upgrade like your friendly computer does. These memory pictures record everything without your conscious control. There are scientists who are exploring this system of memory storage and there are as many arguments about the actual process as there are scientists exploring the phenomenon.

It is not our intention in THE POSITIVE STRESS FACTOR to explain this wondrous system. It is only our intention to suggest to you that this system is retrievable. That this system is accessible to you. You can remember how to start your automobile, can't you? How do you think you do that? You were not born knowing how to drive. There are driving teachers out there who can attest to that! There are no born drivers! We learn and we can retrieve the learned information when we need it.

Why can't we retrieve all of our memory information whenever we want? We believe that the key to that answer is in the energy system and the way in which it works to protect us from the bombardment of the information we store. Some of that information is very painful. How would you like to remember every toothache you ever had in vivid detail? Would you enjoy reliving every cut, bruise, burn, or surgical incision you ever experienced?

How about remembering every unkind word ever spoken to you or every practical joke that you did not find as funny as the joker did? Would you really like to relive the emotions of grief, destructive anger, and rejection every day of your life without end? Perhaps some of us who fall into catatonic states or clinical depression actually do relive, recall, and remember every last detail of a life which was too painful, too vivid, or too overwhelming.

The mind and the body protect us every minute we live. You do not touch a hot surface after you have once burned yourself. You avoid people who hurt you emotionally or physically, if you can. This is a concept we call the "prime directive."

THE "PRIME DIRECTIVE" OF THE ENERGY SYSTEM

In our sessions over the years, we have seen many people whose systems shut down at the first sign of an uncomfortable situation being relived. This protection which we all have does a great job helping us to survive day to day. One of our clients had dealt with severe physical and emotional abuse as a young child. He had been brutalized by a stepmother who tortured her stepchildren when they misbehaved. The memories of those abuses were too violent for the young man to relive. Anytime those memories were recalled, he would become withdrawn and stare into space. He was unable to communicate the emotional and mental anguish of his experience verbally.

His system chose to shut down until, through a long series of sessions, he learned to take away piece after piece of the experiences. If he had not done this, the anger within him would have spilled into his world as violence. Violence is a lesson well taught to many children through abuse. As adults, they will often react as they were treated when they had no power. They will become violent. As a youngster, our client wanted desperately to fight back, but his system's prime directive for self preservation slowed him down until he could deal more easily with the emotional torrent pouring from him.

The prime directive is explained as the individual's natural defense system whose constant purpose is to defend and protect the person, no matter what. In medicine the concept is sometimes called "auto-amputation." The theory of auto-amputation is that in order to preserve the life of the person, the brain will shut down systems which are not necessary to living. If you get a cold, the first system which shuts down, or tries to, is the muscular system. The muscles start to

61

ache and you get tired because you literally do not have to be up walking around to live. You can live lying down. Isn't that right?

The energy required to walk around actually takes away from the energy you need to fight the cold. In order to preserve some of that energy, the brain transfers the energy or "power" to other systems which are more important to the survival of the rest of the body than the muscles. In this way, more energy is channeled into the immune system to restore health. If the cold becomes worse, the brain can shut down more systems. The next system to shut down is usually the digestive system and you become very disinterested in food. Your stomach slows down the digestion of foods in order to transfer energy to the rest of the body fighting the cold. Your elimination system causes diarrhea so that the system is better able to handle the "war" on the cold.

As the system becomes more and more engaged in the war on the cold, the kidneys, lungs, and the rest of the system shut down. As you can guess by now, the prime directive is survival. The prime directive is that the individual physical body must continue to function by channeling the energy it needs to the most vital parts of the system. Finally, the system will shut down everything and die. If we support the system and take over some of the functions to preserve life, the natural defenses can concentrate on other areas. This is why we call it "life support." It is not "life replacement"; it is "support" for the natural defenses which need just that, support to survive.

This prime directive may seem rather ruthless, but without it, an individual could conceivably die from a simple burn or cut or a common cold. In fact, if there is an interference with the natural defense system of the person we can see a simple infection actually cause someone's death. The destruction of the immune system has dire consequences as we all know in this day of AIDS and other immune deficiency diseases. The natural defenses of the body are vital to its health and well-being. The natural defense of the entire energy system allows it to function intelligently and competently throughout many years of stress, frustration, and disappointments.

Without the prime directive for survival, the human individual cannot survive long. Without food, we cannot live long. Without water, we cannot live even a shorter time. Without oxygen, we cannot live for more than a few minutes. The prime directive protects us by using the energy of our lives to direct our survival.

As you can see, energy in all of its forms is the basis of survival. But, do you just want to survive? Wouldn't a life of mere survival be dull? We have the capability to do so much more than just survive. We can learn. We can enjoy. We can challenge ourselves and we can achieve. We can teach others. We can succeed.

EMPOWERMENT FROM ENERGY

Now, we come to the real message of THE POSITIVE STRESS FACTOR. Survival is not the only option for some of us. We who want to achieve, enjoy, and succeed want to use the basic energy we have naturally to protect, preserve, and defend ourselves through life to do even more. We want to use that energy to understand, to grow, and to become the best we can be.

The positive use of stress opens the door to understanding and growth so that we can achieve, enjoy, and succeed. The secret of this approach is not magic or voodoo. We simply use the natural mechanism of the prime directive to achieve more than survival. We use that energy to unlock as much of our potential as is possible. We can learn about that energy system and then use it to open all the doors of possibility. We can use that energy to explain stress and how we can use stress as an asset. We can use the negative and unpleasant experiences of our lives to learn positive lessons. The positive use of stress is another way of saying that any experience can be positive if we know how to use it that way.

Energy Dynamics[R] can take you beyond the basics of living to the extraordinary ability to use your stress, your anger, your fears, and your experiences positively. The "positive stress factor" is the use of stress to achieve more success. Stress can be a signal for you to learn

63

something about yourself you didn't consciously know before. Stress is not something to get rid of forever. It is something to use as a gateway into success and achievement never dreamed possible. "Managing stress" is a common phrase today. *Why do you want to manage something when in fact you can control it? Why do you want to manage stress when you can use it to become more empowered to do what you want to do with your life?*

"Empowerment" is a big word in some circles these days. What does the word mean? To empower yourself means to give yourself power in some form. When you do this, you can then use that power to achieve what you wish. The tool we use in Energy Dynamics^R for that empowerment is the energy of stress. The same energy we have talked about here can be used to give you some power you don't have now. The power can then be used to your advantage in work, play, relationships, creativity, and well-being. Power must be controlled to be constructive. But uncontrolled, power can be destructive. Think about using your energy system to find constructive power for yourself.

The ideas in THE POSITIVE STRESS FACTOR are not all new. Years ago, Norman Vincent Peale talked about the power of positive thinking in our lives. We all know that positive thinking can help us achieve unbelievable things. But, does just thinking positive thoughts give us power?

If you are ready to explore all of the possibilities we just outlined, continue reading. The empowerment we are talking about does not come from anyone but yourself. You can do whatever you want if you know how. Energy Dynamics^R can give you some ideas about how to do this. It is not the only answer, but it is a possibility. Do you want to be a tumbleweed and have no possibilities? Or, do you want to know all of your possibilities and choose the one for you? *It is your choice.*

*"If you have built castles in the air,
your work need not be lost; that is where they should be.
Now put foundations under them."*

Henry David Thoreau

F I V E

THE POWER OF PHYSICAL ENERGY

If you have decided not to be a tumbleweed person, welcome to your first step. We have spent a great deal of time talking about the physical body in relationship to stress. We all know we have a body, but very few of us know that much about it. Your body is really a reflection of how you have treated it over the years. Your body is the first thing that someone notices about you, whether you like it or not. It is the first step in learning how to turn stress into an asset.

DIETS AND NUTRITION

Say the word, "nutrition," and what do most people think? Diet, vitan ins, exercise, minerals, the "basic food groups". Nutrition as a subject strikes fear into the hearts of most people if we mention it in a vacuum. Nutrition is something that most of us never think about until there is a problem. Nutrition belongs in that class of subjects most of us associate with academic pursuits instead of real life.

As a matter of fact, most of us never think about the effects of various foods on our systems until we have a bad reaction. Food and drink are not just substances for survival, they can be the enhancements to the energy system. Foods which we take for granted can be detrimental or supportive to us. Who ever thinks about the effects of the foods we put into our bodies? Do you know how that coffee you had with your breakfast affected your morning? Do you know how that sugar in your tea affects your thinking process? Did you ever think about the long-term effects of our society's eating habits? Of course, many of us are thinking about it today.

We have read about balanced diets and good nutrition for years. We know that a diet of only fast food is not balanced and should be avoided. We know that preservatives and various additives are harmful in large amounts. There are tons of nutrition and diet books on the market today filled with information about what we put into our bodies. Some of the information is very well researched and very soundly based. Some of the information is untested. Some of the writers of these books are, in fact, experts and do have the answers to some degree. But, how do you know the difference between the correct and the incorrect? Between the phony and the scientific? Between the sane and the dangerous?

There are dozens of people willing to advise you on diet and nutrition. There are some who make their living criticizing the works of others and warning us about the dangers of the unproven theories. Many times these warnings are appropriate and should be heeded. Some of these warnings are unfounded because the theory is new and will eventually be proven some day. There are those who have vested interests in some theory or the other and will warn you about theories in which they have no personal investment. Are you to take all of this advice literally and without question?

Do you take everything you read in this book literally? Do you question the theories you are reading here? We certainly hope so. *That is the point!* You should read as much as you can from whatever sources you can find. You should become an expert yourself in *YOU*. No one can describe the perfect diet or the perfect lifestyle for you. You are the only one with all of the information necessary to make those decisions. You are unique and that uniqueness is something which you have a responsibility to understand. The basis of good nutrition is what the effect of the food and drink you consume has on you. Learn to monitor the changes your body makes and the signals your body sends you about those changes. Learn how and what to eat to make yourself feel good and productive.

The diet "rage" in the world has spread its tentacles into practically every family. The impact of society's "accepted" sizes and weights has caused an explosion in the personal image business. Diet books by the millions are produced every year. People spent millions, if not billions, of dollars on health club memberships, retreats, diet pills, and personal trainers. Our young people set their sights on the "perfect body." Thin is in and "fat" is definitely out. It has not always been so. In other cultures and in other times, the well-endowed figure was admired and preserved in painting and sculpture as the ideal.

But, what has all this done to us? We no longer think of food as a pleasure. We are obsessed with what we eat. We are told what to eat and what not to eat. The "cholesterol" police lurk around every corner. The diet gurus have separated us into camps. Some will "never touch" red meat. Some "real" people eat "real" food. Some dieters cringe when the word "fat" is even mentioned in their presence. Some would not be caught eating ice cream, even though they are "dying" for some! We have been brainwashed into our eating habits. We have forgotten our instincts for eating.

Our animal companions usually do a much better job of making nutritional choices than we. Have you ever watched a dog or cat who is ill try to find something in the yard or woods to eat? The purpose, if the animal is allowed to roam free, is to find an anecdote for the substance which he or she has just eaten. In our modern society, our animal companions have been so spoiled that much of the instinctual habits have been counteracted. The modern animal companion is usually not permitted to be instinctual.

A good friend, a doctor of veterinary medicine, becomes incensed when discussing the feeding habits of those humans with the responsibility of an animal companion. He often gets on his "soapbox" about people feeding their animals "people" food and trying to make those animals fit into the society's idea of what is good nutrition. You see, a dog's nutritional needs are not yours. Neither are your needs like your dog's. Neither are your needs like any other human.

You are unique and you must learn about that uniqueness from the understanding of the human energy system. The basis of life is the sustaining of that life. The prime directive for the energy system is to sustain life and preserve all of the functioning parts of that life. What better way to begin than to talk about the basic need for food? An old professor of Dr. Holmes's once ended a lecture on nutrition by saying, "Remember, if you wear out your body, where are you going to live?" Where do you intend to live if your physical body is destroyed?

THE ENERGY OF FOOD

Feeding the physical body is not just necessary, it is vital. Let's talk a little about the use of food and way in which that food affects the whole system. We are not going to go into a discussion of basic physiology and the process of digestion and assimilation. We want to talk about the role of the food within the whole system. We want to give you an idea about the way in which you can use your own system to learn about food choices. You will not become an expert by reading this book, but you will, at least, be able to think a little more about your system's changes and what caused those changes.

Let's begin with the basics of how the system identifies and makes decisions about foods. On a very simple level, the human brain has been programmed to recognize everything that enters the system and everything that is produced within the system. The brain does this by comparing a substance with a "model" or "template" stored within its memory. The brain doesn't recognize food by name like we do when we see it, but the brain does recognize food by its chemical and physical structure. When a food is ingested, the brain must decide many things about that food.

First of all, it must decide if the food is palatable. In order to do this, the brain and its nervous system network take the information supplied by the mouth, the nose, and the eyes and compare that information to what is already stored in the memory. As an illustration, let's go back to our friendly computer. If the computer is programmed to recognize commands and signals from the keyboard, the computer will respond. We all laugh about the expression, "it does not compute," when someone does not understand what someone else has said. If the computer does not understand, it will not respond until it has more information.

Once again, the human system is more complex than the computer. If the human system does not recognize a command or a substance, the brain can analyze it and make a decision about what to do next. There are several options available to the brain and the human energy system. If the substance you just put into your mouth is recognized immediately, the brain will send the appropriate messages to various systems. The other systems will then do their jobs and digest the food properly. But, what if there is a problem at that first step?

You already know the answer, don't you? Haven't you ever had the experience of looking into your refrigerator and wondering just exactly what that substance was hiding in that plastic container? You smell it. You poke at it with your finger. You analyze it visually. If you are really brave, you taste it. What if that substance doesn't pass the tests? You know when something is spoiled, don't you? You can smell, taste, and sometimes, see that it is. The human brain does the same thing without you knowing it most of the time. Your brain makes decisions about food constantly. The food is either accepted or rejected based on a massive investigation by all of your senses. If the food is obviously inedible, it does not get into your mouth. Or, if it does, it doesn't stay long.

If the food is eaten, perhaps it has a delayed rejection by the system. The food may come right back out because the brain has recognized that it is harmful. The brain may also know that the system cannot handle any more food and rejects it. Either way, the body rids itself of something which the brain determines it does not need. This is a long winded way of saying that the brain is constantly monitoring what you eat and drink, making decisions, and rejecting what is dangerous or unnecessary.

The brain at its most basic functioning level does its job rather effectively. But, what happens when the brain's prime directive is overridden? What happens when we think we "know" better about what we should eat? We can override the system. We can eat too much. We can eat things which are not exactly nourishing and good for us. We can make some really dangerous decisions. And, most of us do all the time.

Have you ever had the feeling that you should stop eating? Have you ever had the feeling that what you were eating was not a good idea? No? Well, you have learned how to override the system rather successfully, haven't you? You can eat anything in any quantity and ignore the prime directive . . . *and you have!* We have taught our systems to override common sense in many things. We, as a society, often choose unwisely. We drink too much alcohol. We eat too much fat. We eat too much sugar. We eat *beyond need to gluttony!*

As a modern society, we have successfully decided that we "know" best. We choose to make decisions not based on survival, but based on other needs. We drink some substances to forget. We eat some foods to do the same thing. We choose to eat to cure a multitude of emotional difficulties. The old expression, "you are what you eat," can easily be translated into a new expression, "you eat to be what you are not." We all know that there are times when food is the friend we don't have. Food can become the companion who won't reject us. Food can remind us of a happier day or a happier situation. Food can be a substitute for many things. Food can also be the enemy.

In a situation called "bulimia" the love/hate relationship with food is violently obvious. Several of the clients we have worked with over the years have faced the pain of eating disorders which have controlled them for many reasons. Food had become both an enemy and a friend. The substitutions we make with foods are monstrous at times and cause great difficulties.

THE ABUSE OF FOOD FOR ENERGY

Cassandra was one of those bright young women on her way up. She had fought to be exactly what she thought was the successful image for the young female executive. In order to be the image, Cassandra had learned a powerful tool to keep thin. As many women and men have learned, bulimia is a kind of solution. Cassandra was working on her MBA and her goal was within reach, but there was one problem. She was not just thin anymore. She was a walking skeleton. No one would hire anyone like her.

Like most people dealing with such a problem, weight was not the real issue. Self-esteem and self-acceptance were the real culprits for Cassandra. She really could not remember any specific incidents or events which caused this low self-esteem. She was the perfect daughter and a good student. She had many friends who responded well to her. But, Cassandra was her worst critic. She could not see the fun-loving and likable person she really was. All Cassandra saw was someone who was fat and ugly. She only saw someone who was not quite "good enough."

Cassandra began to get her bulimia under control when she recognized that she had an extreme sense of failure. She thought of herself as a bonsai tree with many bristly and sharp branches. It was a strong tree, but it needed a place to grow. The message of the bonsai tree was that she was constantly adapting to others' definitions of what she was to be instead of growing naturally.

During one particular recollection from the past, Cassandra remembered an incident with her father in which, while she talked, her father read the newspaper. The memory was quite vivid, and she recalled how that feeling of rejection was something she translated into her other dealings with men in particular. The only way to get attention was to be the perfect shape and size. Cassandra's "eating

71

disorder" was not an eating disorder at all. She was a young vital woman whose energy system was unbalanced by the way she had interpreted the use of food. Food was definitely an enemy which contributed to her image of herself as ugly and fat. In some strange way, the bulimia was a double-edged blessing for Cassandra. It protected her. It insulated her from the stress of rejection. It was also her salvation. It led her to examine the causes of her low self-worth.

Without the stress factors, Cassandra would not have been forced into such a situation. She used that stress to find answers to her search for an identity which was not dependent upon others for verification.

Even if the situation is not as destructive as "bulimia," we all suffer to some degree from the misuse of our food choices. Often, we do not realize the effect of our food choices until we change our habits. If we isolate our choices and habits, we can examine them. A young boy was once brought to Dr. Webb for a psychological evaluation because he was having a great deal of difficulty at school and home. He was doing poorly with his studies, and he was becoming violent at home with his siblings. The mother of the young boy had come to the end of her rope and was searching everywhere for a solution to the problem.

As with many such children, or adults for that matter, when an obvious organic difficulty is not discovered, people will seek out the psychologists. Obviously, they feel that the problem must be "in your head." Sometimes, they are exactly right and the problem's solution is not to be found in the organic systems. Sometimes, the mind is the key to the problem. In this case, the young boy did not have any obvious physical problem and the mother was sent to the psychologist to find a "psychological" solution.

The boy's antisocial and aggressive behavior were becoming serious as time went on and the psychological solutions did not seem to be adequate. One day, the young boy told Dr. Webb that he had stopped at a fast food restaurant on the way to the office. She asked him if he did that often, and he said, "Yeah, I love to go there, but

Mom doesn't take me there very much." He talked about his love of French fries, milkshakes, and other snacks. He talked about his choices of breakfast foods and how much he loved chocolate.

As the session went on, Dr. Webb wondered if perhaps some of the problems he was having could be connected to the large amount of sugar he was consuming every day. She asked his mother. The mother was extremely upset by the question because she felt that she was very careful about the diet choices she made. She could not imagine that his diet was poor, and she could not imagine how she could make it better. Dr. Webb was equally adamant and suggested that the mother take a survey of the amount of sugars her son ate during the week.

After a week had passed, the mother came to Dr. Webb and reported that she was absolutely amazed at the amount of sugar consumed by her son throughout the week. She had been surprised to find that his diet was so unbalanced. *That was the point!* It was not exactly what he was eating, but *how* unbalanced his eating was. The foods he ate were, in and of themselves, not detrimental. The fact that he had such an unbalanced diet was the important factor. The sugars did not directly cause his behavior, but because the sugars were not balanced by other food choices his system was put into an unbalanced situation. Stress was the result. Stress was caused by the imbalance in his diet. The stress symptoms he exhibited were irritability, uncontrolled anger, frustration, and irrational behaviors. He was also showing signs of improper rest. He was cranky and hard to handle at home and in school. His memory was affected and he could not achieve in his school work.

What do you do once you have identified a possible problem? The simplest choice is to go back to square one, eliminate everything from the diet which is questionable, and then, start to make changes in the diet adding one food at a time. This is what the boy's mother did. She eliminated all sugars for about a week to ten days. Then, she slowly and methodically added some sugars, one at a time. She watched for reactions and avoided those foods which caused an adverse reaction. In this way, she found that her son's behaviors were affected by certain sugars, but not all. The boy's behavior changed dramatically over the next few weeks. His school work improved. He quit getting into trouble at school and fighting with his brothers and sisters as much. In general, the changes were quite obvious to everyone. Most dramatically, the changes were obvious to the young boy himself. He actually would refuse to eat certain foods because he "didn't want to get into trouble at school" the next day. He knew that he was a different person and he somehow knew that the changes in his diet created changes in the way he interacted with his world.

The results of this one incident led us to explore the implications of diet with other clients. The reactions that people have to certain foods are fairly clear in some cases. Most of us know which foods and drinks cause us problems. But, what happens when we are not consciously aware of the effects of these choices? Many of us are so out of touch with our systems that we don't connect what we eat with how we feel. The basis for understanding diet's impact on our energy systems is understanding the energy system itself and then, respecting its power. If we are truly aware of the effects of foods, drinks, and other tangible contacts we have, we can monitor the changes those contacts cause.

Can you imagine what your days would be like if you were aware of the effects of certain foods and drinks immediately as you consume them? When you feel a bit under the weather for no apparent reason, how do you usually react? Do you wait until it gets worse before you pay attention? Do you think that it will just pass if you wait long enough? Do you wonder to yourself if what you feel is the beginning of something serious? Do you ask advice? Do you ignore what you feel? Do any of these reactions sound familiar?

Of course, they do. There is probably no one reading this book who has not had at least one of these reactions from time to time. We notice reactions in our bodies and minds all of the time. Sometimes those reactions are so subtle that we can "keep on going" without any changes. There was at one time a commercial advertising a famous cold remedy. The point of the commercial was that if you felt the first signs of a cold, taking this remedy would keep you on your feet so that your life could continue without inconvenience.

The message was very clear. If you are feeling a bit worn out and tired, don't stop what you need to do. Take a remedy which will allow you to continue in spite of the warnings. If your system is trying to tell you something, just bypass the signal and go on. This is very much like turning off the fire alarm instead of putting out the fire. The reason you have a fire alarm is to alert you to danger. There is little point in turning off the alarm when it signals you without attending to the reason for the alarm in the first place. Doesn't make much sense, does it?

LEARNING TO USE THE ENERGY OF FOOD

Through Energy Dynamics[R], we give people an opportunity to monitor the effects of various foods and drinks we consume every day. The effects of these substances can be seen quickly in a seminar session. The impact on the energy system is very obvious. A special muscle test is used to demonstrate the effect sugars have on the physical body. A volunteer tastes different sugars and sugar substitutes and we observe the impact on his or her body. Not only is the body affected by the test, but sometimes, even the conscious mental functions are affected. The volunteers we have tested over the years have reported all kinds of effects.

One person noted that after tasting a small amount of granulated sugar, she experienced a slight dizziness. Another reported a slight headache. Yet another told us that he was feeling a bit nauseous after eating a small amount of a sugar substitute widely used today. Some persons had minimal reactions to the sugars, but they all had some reaction. We surmised that the differences came from the tolerance of each person to the substance being tested. If someone was very much accustomed to sugar, the reaction was not as strong. If someone was not a sugar consumer, the reaction was usually more obvious.

If the system had grown accustomed to the consumption of certain foods, those foods did not seem to cause the more obvious reactions. The energy system is a miracle of adaptation. It learns very quickly how to survive. In the early part of this century, the cure for venereal disease was measured doses of poison. The poison was used much as certain chemotherapy drugs are used today. Some of these substances can be lethal in the wrong dosages, but in measured amounts under supervision the effect is beneficial. The human energy system can adapt and does routinely every minute of every day.

But, what does all this mean to you and your everyday life? If we can observe that a minute amount of a certain food will cause a reaction, then why can't that we learn to sense those reactions every day and learn from them. In an isolated situation, we are all very observant. Try an experiment right now.

Sit back and get comfortable.

Did you move in any way? Did you shift your body into a different position? Did you feel yourself change in any way? Why? Weren't you comfortable for the last ten minutes? Did you just realize that you weren't comfortable when you were asked to "get comfortable?" Why weren't you monitoring your system better before you were asked to monitor it? Weren't you suddenly aware of your body? Why weren't you aware of it before you were forced to be?

Interesting questions? Think about them a little while longer.

"Believe nothing,
no matter where you read it,
or who said it--
even if I have said it--
unless it agrees with your own reason
and your own common sense."

The Buddha

Think Bite #5

Are you tired of thinking? O.k., let's call this a "non-think bite." It's going to be a "feel bite." We want you to feel something about your body. Remember those stress points we talked about earlier? If you don't remember, it's fine. You're not supposed to be thinking in this segment anyway.

We'll take one stress point at a time. Now, sit back and relax. Take a deep breath like you've been practicing and just relax. Now, concentrate on your body and just feel what is going on in it. Close your eyes for a few seconds if that helps and feel your body. Sort of explore your body with your mind and just feel where there might be a slight discomfort or a little ache or pain. Where do you feel it?

The place you feel that little discomfort is a stress point. Maybe it's a place you have felt before. Maybe it's a new place for you. Anyway, as you focus on that stress point, take a deep breath. Pause for a few seconds and feel the tension rise as you hold your breath. Feel that tension like a power buildup in your system. Now, think about that stress point.

Let your breath out and relax. Try it again. Breathe in, pause, let the tension build, focus on that stress point, and breathe out. Simple. Try this experiment several times during the day. You'll find that the stress points sometimes change. You may discover you have more than one point. Try to concentrate on the most uncomfortable one at a time.

What do you feel after you do this a couple of times? Is the stress point you first felt still uncomfortable? Has it changed in any way? How does your body feel compared to what it felt like a few minutes ago?

This is the first step in getting to know your own energy system. When you can become aware of your physical body, you can then become aware of the rest of your system. Many of us go through our lives ignoring the signs and signals our bodies give us every day. We pay more attention to our cars and trucks than we do our bodies. When you hear a strange noise under the hood of your car, you take it to a mechanic. When your VCR is making strange noises, you have it checked. When the dishwasher is acting up, you pay attention.

Why don't you pay as much attention to your own body? After all, you live in it every day. Do you know it very well? A few years ago, there were two books published with interesting titles. They were WOMAN'S BODY: AN OWNER'S MANUAL and MAN'S BODY: AN OWNER'S MANUAL. Have you read the owner's manual for your own body lately? You can just by paying attention to the signals and using your energy system to listen to those signals.

POSITIVE AWARENESS OF YOUR ENERGY SYSTEM

The positive use of energy is the awareness of your current situation. It is just that simple. If you become aware of your system, you can make changes quickly and effectively. Why wait for someone to tell you to get comfortable? Why wait for someone to tell you that you look tired? Why wait for someone to tell you how to change your lifestyle? Why wait?

We are not suggesting that we should all throw out everything in our kitchens which contain sugar. We are not suggesting that foods are ruining your life. We are not suggesting that we should all give up coffee or chocolate. We are suggesting that you take stock of your own reactions to the foods, medicines, herbs, vitamins, drinks, and other substances you use and monitor your own energy system. The burden of proof is not with your doctor, pharmacist, spouse, neighbor, friendly neighborhood herbalist or self-proclaimed holistic practitioner. In the final analysis, your body depends on you to make decisions which are informed and judicious.

There was a man who had a piece of pie every day of his life for breakfast, lunch, and dinner. *Before his meal. Every day of his life he had his big piece of pie.* He lived well into his eighties without ever having a sick day in his life. There was another woman who ate at least a half gallon of ice cream daily until she was 92 years of age. *It is also rumored that she smoked a cigar after dinner each evening.* By the way, she was killed in an automobile accident.

But, there is also the story of a young man of 9 who was a high achiever in school. He was having trouble every day before school losing his breakfast and anything else he ate in the morning. He was painfully thin. He was jaundiced. He had a distended abdomen. He was a sick little boy. His parents were completely baffled because the hospital could find "nothing wrong" with him. It was determined that he was afraid of failure and was avoiding school by being sick every day. When he was placed on a strict diet which included no red meat, no refined sugars, and no soft drinks, however, he began to change his habits. He gained weight, began eating everything in sight, and eventually became a 6 foot tall, 170 pound, well-muscled young man. The problem was not totally psychological, but because there was no overt tissue damage yet, the physical was not explored. If his parents had watched what he was eating and if they knew what effects those foods could have to throw him off balance, he could have been spared many months of illness.

Think Bite #6

This is a "bite bite" actually. In this segment, we want you to think about your diet. There's that "word" again. No, we don't want you to berate yourself about your weight or your bad eating habits. We don't want you to brag about your good eating habits either. In this bite you are going to do what so many of us should do if we are serious about our physical well being.

Take one week and write down everything that you eat during that week. Be honest with yourself. Write down *everything*. No one is going to send this list to any government agency or to any blackmailer. It is for your eyes only. After you have done this, what do you see? Is your diet balanced? Is it balanced not just from the standpoint of "proper" nutritional choices, but from the perspective of a balance of foods?. Is there an abundance of one type of food? What is the balance of sugar to proteins in your diet? How much coffee and tea are you drinking in an average day?

Are you surprised? Most of us do not realize what we are eating most of the time. Only when we "go on a diet", do we notice such things. If there is an abundance of sugar in your diet, try an experiment. Cut the sugar out for one week. *Cut it all out!* Don't use any sugar substitutes either. For one week, do without the sugar.

Now, there is a caution here. If you begin to have headaches or other side effects, be careful. If you in fact do have headaches or other effects, you probably have an addiction or dependency to the food. Don't be surprised or frightened by it. Just increase your water intake and increase your supplies of fruits to get some natural sugars in place of the granulated kinds.

If you see that coffee is a excessive part of your diet, cut it out. Many people will tell us that when they do cut out the coffee they actually go through a withdrawal. We both did when we decided to eliminate caffeine from our diets. The greater the dependence on the substance, the more intense the reaction when you quit. But, remember, this is an experiment. You will never know what your body's reaction to a substance is unless you isolate it for a while.

If you have a medical problem for which this experiment may be dangerous, please don't try it. If you are on medications for diabetes for instance, the diet alterations must be carefully monitored. But, if you are relatively healthy and not known to have any particular medical difficulties, the experiment will not harm you. The human body is a miracle of adaptation. Rest and a good diet can do wonders to bring you back into balance. Don't worry about all those B movies in which the addict spends days and nights in withdrawal trying to "dry out." There are no horror stories here. Just begin to notice the differences that changes in diet can make.

One rather harmless dietary experiment you can try easily is to increase your intake of water. This does not mean all "fluid" intake. It means water intake. Many people will try to increase water intake by drinking more iced tea, coffee, soft drinks, or juices. When we say "water", we mean water. The average person does not drink enough water a day as a general rule. The increase in water can cause a great difference in the way your energy system processes its energy. The body retains water in the soft tissues if you do not drink enough, so to take away that "bloated" feeling, perhaps water is the answer. Only you can judge. Try it. Drink more water a day and observe your body's changes.

Diet and other physical supports for your own body are your choices. Little babies and young children cannot make those choices for themselves, but you can. You have a choice. Make it.

THE MIX OF PHYSICAL AND EMOTIONAL ENERGY

Nutrition and diet are the cornerstones of a complex system which needs care. That system based on energy thrives on good fuel, proper management of that fuel, and the wise use of the energy it produces. The old expression, "Garbage in; garbage out," takes on a whole new meaning when we think of our whole energy system. Diet is the mainstay of a balanced system. A balanced system is unstressed. An unstressed system is efficient. An efficient system is successful.

The connection between the foods we eat and the emotional stability we all can have was demonstrated to us recently by one very bright client. Sam had been experiencing anxiety attacks for several months before seeing us. He was dealing with a death in his family and the ramifications of that death. He was terrified that he might also suffer a sudden death even though Sam was a healthy young man.

The experience of the recent death brought back memories of other deaths which were sudden and unexpected. Sam struggled for months with his feelings of terror and anxiety. The anxiety began to affect his work and he became more and more anxious about his future. Sam began his sessions in Energy Dynamics[R] and did learn a great deal about why his reactions were so strong. He had dreams about his own death, and Sam felt that his family would be devastated if he were to die suddenly. He also felt that he had not really begun to live and was not ready to face his own mortality.

As he continued his sessions, Sam cleared away many of his fears and anxieties, but the anxiety attack symptoms continued. He said that he had tried on several occasions to quit smoking, but to no avail. We told him that the nicotine in the cigarettes might be contributing to his feelings and symptoms. Sam was willing to try anything and gave up the cigarettes.

The anxiety symptoms lessened and Sam felt wonderful. He was amazed at the changes he had accomplished, and he was quite pleased that his sessions had been so successful. He left the clinic with a new outlook on life.

Do you think that this was the last we heard from Sam? No. Sam had confronted some of his problems, but he had not really taken the responsibility of monitoring his own system yet. He quit the smoking because we had told him that the cigarettes *might be contributing* to his symptoms. He did not make any connection between the physical reality of the drug, nicotine, on his entire energy system. To Sam, the anxiety attacks were purely emotional responses based on some fears and terror he harbored. When the reasons for the fears were known, in Sam's mind, the problem was solved.

Months went by and nothing was heard from or about Sam. One day, he appeared in the clinic. He had been having a terrible time with new symptoms. Sam was convinced that we had not helped "cure" him of the attacks and he was right back where he started. He was sure that he was going to suffer a breakdown from which there would be no rescue. Sam told us how his work was suffering and how his personal life was being changed. His wife was worried about him and a little annoyed that he was so preoccupied with his condition.

Sam reported that he had changed nothing in his life. He was still looking for someone or something to "cure" him. After several sessions, he felt no better and was very discouraged. In passing, Sam told us that he was still not smoking, but had found a substitute for the cigarette craving. He was *chewing tobacco instead of smoking it.* The idea that tobacco in any form might be contributing to his physical condition was something that Sam never imagined. When we told him that the same effect of the cigarettes could be experienced with the chewing tobacco, he was not convinced. He was sure that the cause of his symptoms was emotional. How could what he was chewing and not swallowing actually affect his emotional stability?

To make a very long story a bit shorter, we once again coerced Sam into quitting his tobacco habit. Many weeks afterward, Sam visited us and was so thankful that he was feeling better. He told us, "I don't know what you did, but I feel great." He still had not accepted the fact that his own system was trying to help him. His system was reacting to the nicotine in such a way as to cause the symptoms of the nervous attacks. Nicotine for Sam was the culprit, not necessarily because nicotine is a "bad" drug, but that Sam's system could not assimilate the drug effectively. Smoking and chewing for Sam were the contributing factors to cause his system to be unbalanced and stressed. When that happened, all of the emotional and mental trauma he suffered became more acute. In our society, the idea that the mind and the body are so intricately connected with one another is not widely understood or accepted. The intimate connection between our physical body and the mind is still uncharted territory for most of us.

THE FOUNDATION OF THE ENERGY SYSTEM

Nutrition is a complex subject when we only think of the rules and guidelines that someone has designated for us. The rules of good nutrition and good diet are not complex if we rely on our own systems to teach us what is good and what is not. Listen to your own system and recognize that what you put into your body will affect, not just your body, but your mind and emotions as well. The truth of Energy Dynamics[R] is that the energy of the system is continuous. We are the result of what we eat and drink.

Energy begins with fuel and the fuels the human energy system uses may be foods, water, air, or thoughts. It doesn't really matter what fuel we are discussing, the energy of that fuel must be used by the system in some way. As the owner of your own energy system, you can monitor it and use it in any way you wish. It is really up to you to, not only listen to advice about your nutritional needs, but also listen to your own system. When you feel a little unbalanced, learn to check into your system and analyze what may have caused the problem. After all, you live in your body, don't you? You probably know that body better than anyone else ever could. At least, you should know it that well. If you don't, you have some work to do. You owe it to yourself and all those who care about you to make the most of your energy system. Use it as it was intended. Give your system a chance by looking at all the options available to you.

"The soul . . .
never thinks without a picture."

Aristotle

SIX

THE POWER OF MEMORY

Every day, when Maggie drove to her office, she hesitated in the parking lot before she walked into the building. Maggie was one the best office managers in the city. She was very efficient, very competent, and very happy . . . *most of the time.* There was a problem though. You see, Maggie had a supervisor who could not let one day go by without making Maggie feel like a complete failure. Every time Maggie had a one on one conference with her supervisor, Eleanor, she came away from the meeting feeling incompetent, inefficient, and unhappy.

Eleanor was one of those powerfully strong willed people who have the ability to make those around them lose confidence. There was just something about the way Eleanor talked to Maggie that destroyed all the confidence that Maggie otherwise had most of the time. There was some button Eleanor could press in Maggie that made Maggie quake. Maggie had attended one of our seminars for middle managers and during a break, she asked us for some advice. She was miserable at work. She loved her job most of the time, but the problem with Eleanor had caused her so much anxiety that now she hated work. She found herself having what she called "anxiety attacks" just thinking about going to work.

We asked Maggie how she had handled the situation in the past. She told us that when she knew she would see Eleanor, Maggie tried to empty herself of all of the emotion she could. She tried not to think about anything. She thought about nothing. She wanted to be neutral when she talked to Eleanor. As a result, she went into her meetings with "an empty energy bucket."

THE "ENERGY BUCKET"

Every day each of us starts our days with an "energy bucket", and we can fill that bucket with whatever we wish. We can fill it with positive or negative thoughts or no thoughts at all. If we fill it with nothing at all, then all day long, with every encounter we have, the energy bucket is filled with the experiences and impressions from everything we do and everyone we meet. Without making a choice about what is in your energy bucket, you are letting others fill it for you.

This is exactly what Maggie was doing. She emptied her bucket and Eleanor could fill it with all the negative thoughts and impressions she wanted. Now, Eleanor probably did not know she was doing this. She didn't know about impacting others that way. The problem was that Maggie didn't understand the impact of others' thoughts either. With an empty energy bucket, Maggie opened herself up, allowing Eleanor to dump all the negative energy on her with no protection. Maggie began to believe that she was incompetent because her energy system had received only Eleanor's thoughts about her.

Maggie wanted to know how to stop this. She said that she had been reading about "positive thinking", and she had tried some of the various self-help techniques on dealing with bosses. None of these seemed to work for her. Maggie was becoming more and more depressed, withdrawn, and frightened of the stress she felt. It was the stress that brought her to the seminar in the first place.

We asked Maggie if she had some favorite place or favorite time that always made her happy. She said, "Oh, yes, it's kind of silly, but on Saturday, when I don't work, I love to snuggle under my grandmother's old down quilt and feel all that warmth around me. I don't have to face the world and I feel safe." Maggie had reached back into her memory storage and chosen an impression which she felt was secure and comfortable. She could actually recall other days with her grandmother when she was a child feeling safe and happy.

We told Maggie to use that memory to fill her energy bucket. We told her to recall that wonderful feeling of warmth and security when she knew she would see Eleanor. We also asked her to tell us what happened the next time she had a meeting with Eleanor.

Several weeks went by and a letter came from Maggie. She was absolutely thrilled to report that there had been this wonderful change in Eleanor. She no longer frightened Maggie and Maggie actually was beginning to feel confident and happy again. She told us that other people in the office noticed the difference and commented on it. They wanted to know what Maggie had done to make the change in Eleanor.

Actually, Eleanor had not changed. At least, she had not changed as much as Maggie. It was Maggie's newfound power that had made the difference. Maggie had filled her bucket with the positive thoughts she had chosen and there was no room for any of Eleanor's negativity. It was a simple exercise, but a powerful lesson for Maggie. It taught her about impressions and how these impressions, stored in her memory, could turn a very stressful situation into a triumph. She was now directing her own power and she was no longer dependent upon Eleanor, or anyone else, to dictate how she felt.

Think Bite #7

Do you want to try an impression recall? Remember you have zillions of memories to recall each day. All of those pictures and impressions are stored for you to use. Some of them are bad and some are good. Let's talk about the good ones. You have lived a long time when you think about the memory storage unit you are. The wise use of these impressions starts by remembering the good memories just as Maggie did.

There is a great quote from one of John-Roger and Peter McWilliams's books credited to Edith Armstrong. "I keep the telephone of my mind open to peace, harmony, health, love, and abundance. Then, whenever doubt, anxiety, or fear try to call me, they get a busy signal--and soon they'll forget my number." Let's see if you can keep the "telephone" of your mind busy with happy memories. Just like the energy bucket you fill every morning, that telephone can carry only the messages you choose.

We want you to close your eyes and go back into your memory unit to choose the happiest day of your life. When you do this, don't try, just do it. Remember the STAR WARS movies? In one of the best of that series, Luke Skywalker is being taught by Yoda, the wise and brave Jedi warrior. As Yoda explains the Jedi philosophy to Luke, Luke becomes argumentative and questions everything that Yoda tries to tell him to do. He says he will "try." Yoda's reply is quite succinct. *"Do or do not. There is no try."*

It is just like this with memory recall. Do or do not. Trying does not work. Remember that your computer brain can recall anything for you. It's just waiting for the question. It's like that little cursor on a computer, blinking and blinking, waiting for you to do something. Now, are you ready?

Remember, with your breath, you have the tension to accomplish anything you want. Breathe in, hold your breath, and think about the happiest day of your life. Breathe out. What did you remember? Did a thought come to you? Did a picture appear in your mind's eye? There are great memories in there to be remembered. All you have to do is DO IT! Now, just as Maggie did, you can use that memory to fill your energy bucket any time you wish. When you are next under a great deal of stress or upset over some project or problem, try this simple experiment. Think of a happy time in your life. When you think of that time, remember all of the detail you can about it to make it very real. If there are sounds associated with it, hear them. If there are scents, smell them. Make that imagined memory vivid, and you can use it to turn stress into a positive for yourself.

MEMORY IMPRESSIONS

Bert Decker discusses the impression we make on audiences as the "stuff of the First Brain." Mr. Decker believes that in order to appeal more effectively to anyone, you must rely on this "First Brain" which is the seat of the emotional impressions in every person. The point about speakers is that when we speak it is neither the precision nor the facts which move our audiences to believe or disbelieve what we say. It is the intangible "impression" we make upon our audience which carries the most weight.

Impressions stored in the memory banks are very important in Energy Dynamics[R.] Impressions are those "pictures" we talked about in a previous chapter. These impressions are stored just like data on a computer disk, *but with one very important difference.* Computers have limits to their memory storage, but the human energy system has an almost infinite memory for us to use.

Impressions are the memories of past experiences complete with all the smells, sounds, sights, feelings, and thoughts we had during the experience itself. These impressions are different than one-dimensional photographs because impressions carry all of the elements which made up the memory experience. To illustrate this idea, we want to tell you a story about a man and a dog.

One day George came home from a hard day at work and all he wanted was a good dinner, a quiet evening at home, and perhaps a little sympathy. George and his wife were not exactly newlyweds but not exactly ready for divorce either. They were like most married couples with a past. They had their quarrels, disagreements, and their differences from time to time. *This was one of those times.* George didn't even know how the argument started. It just did.

After several minutes of heated discussion during which nothing much was accomplished or resolved, George stormed out of the house to walk around the block. He wanted to "cool off." As he was walking around the block, he was thinking . . . thinking about the job stress . . . thinking about the argument . . . thinking about the economy. He was thinking about a great many things. He was also filled with emotion about his latest argument with his wife. Anger, frustration, and helplessness all nested together in his mind and in his memory banks.

As he walked around the block, George's mind was storing all of the experience. *All of the experience* was being recorded in detail. The sights, sounds, feelings, and emotions every second of his walk were indelibly impressed on his memory. Along the way, George passed a neighbor's hedge fence. Suddenly, the neighbor's big dog jumped from behind the fence and grabbed George's leg. Ouch!! George shook the dog and the neighbor called the dog off, but the damage was done. The dog had taken a chunk out of George's leg.

Off to the hospital went George with all his anger, fright, and damage. The wound was cleaned; the appropriate treatments were given, and George went home.

Now, comes the interesting part. A few weeks later, George comes home from work as usual, and again, it has been a bad day for George. He just wants some peace and quiet. He wants his dinner and the evening paper. Once again, George may snap at his wife; she snaps back at him, and another argument ensues. Sound familiar? As the argument progresses, George notices something very strange. His leg is beginning to hurt. It hurts right in the same spot where the dog bit him. Are you surprised? You shouldn't be. The impression stored from the dog bite carries the emotions, sights, sounds, and feelings of that previous experience. The emotions which George felt during the dog bite are permanently impressed with the other physical experience.

THE ENERGY OF THE MEMORY IMPRESSION

Joseph Conrad said, "The mind of man (or woman) is capable of anything - because everything is in it, all the past as well as all the future." The impression is a total picture, not just a flat experience. Imagine that you are looking at a family photo. Some of the people on the photograph you like. Some of the people are not favorites. But, when you look at the photograph, you see everybody, not just the people you *want to see*. You must face the unpleasant as well as the pleasant part of the memory evoked by the photo.

This explains our story about George. The experience of George and the dog was all wrapped up in the emotional environment of the argument with his wife. When one part of the impression is triggered by a memory brought to the surface, the rest of the impression is brought into play again.

George did not realize that the two were connected. As a matter of fact, few people realize the complexity of their memories. This is why we often hear clients say, "I don't know why I said that." The inexplicable can be *explained* by understanding the energy of the memory storage system. We cannot possibly remember consciously all that has happened to us over a lifetime. There are some of us who have been in psychoanalysis for years trying to understand the meanings behind events in our lives. Years of therapy sometimes lead to a conscious understanding of the reasons for some actions, but it is a little like searching for the proverbial "needle in a haystack." You may tear the haystack down bit by bit until you find the needle, but it may take years before it is discovered, and maybe, it will never be discovered at all.

Barbara Streisand was interviewed on TODAY a little more than a year ago. It was one of her rare interviews and Gene Shalit was asking professional questions, but could not resist a few personal ones. Ms. Streisand is a very private person, but agreed to his personal questions. One question was "What do you notice first about a man?" After a slight hesitation, Ms. Streisand replied, "his teeth." To which Mr. Shalit responded, "What?" She laughed and told him why.

She said that when she was young and her mother was dating, she remembered one man who came to take her mother out for the evening. When the man smiled, Ms. Streisand said she noticed the man's teeth. It made a big impression. Ever since, she reported, men's teeth have been barometers for her reaction to them.

The interesting part of this short story is twofold. First, the importance of that impression from her youth which impacted on her for the rest of her life. More importantly perhaps is that after "years" of therapy, she said, she knew why she reacted that way, but she still did react. *Knowing the "why" of the reaction, she said, did not change the reaction.*

THE DIFFERENCE WITH ENERGY DYNAMICS[R]

We have seen many clients over the years with almost exactly the same stories to tell. After years of traditional psychotherapy and analysis, they may know why something bothers them, but they still have the reactions. Nothing has changed about the impression stored in their memories. In order for the reaction to change, there must be a change in the impression which is stored. We cannot change the actual events stored in the memory, but through the energy of the thought process, we can *alter the reaction through changing the emotional connotations stored along with the physical reality of the event!*

Through Energy Dynamics[R,] we can find the needle in the haystack without tearing down the entire stack. We can find the needle in the memory impression of one experience. The needle may hold the key to the reasons why we say the things we do and do the things we do without conscious reasoning. This is not tapping into the unconscious through hypnosis, but rather tapping into the conscious energy system storage. It is that storage which helps us type a letter from the memory of experience. It is that storage which allows us to drive a car from the memory of experience. It is the same storage which we can use to learn why we do and feel certain things. If we can use that energy memory storage, we can achieve success. We can learn to use the stresses we feel as assets instead of liabilities.

Let's get back to George and the dog. Up until now, the connection between the emotional coloring of the experience and the actual physical damage is fairly simple. The complications come in when we consider that the mind just doesn't store information for later retrieval; the mind interprets what it stores.

As we move along having one experience after another, we not only store that information for later use, but our mind also applies some interpretation of events which may or may not be totally accurate. Have there been times when you have had an argument or disagreement with someone which centered on a simple difference in interpretation? Have you ever argued with someone about politics or religion? Do you always have the same interpretations about those things as your friends or loved ones? If you have had nothing but bad experiences with a certain person, group, sex, or nationality, do you think your personal belief system is biased when it comes to that person, group, sex, or nationality?

If you have answered no to those questions, you can stop reading, because you have already cleared your energy system of misinterpretations of the events in your life, and you are completely balanced and in control of your life. Right? If this is not the case, please read on.

George was bitten by the dog, but it wasn't just any dog. It was a German Shepherd. George has nothing against German Shepherds as a breed, but it is interesting that George has had only two experiences with them and on both occasions, he has been bitten. That could make him a little wary about the breed, don't you think? George didn't think so.

George never thought one way or another about the breed of dog he encountered. He did not think about it consciously, but the unconscious connection to the German Shepherd breed was still there in the impression "picture" he had stored. The impressions of both incidents were stored for future use. George had some emotional responses to the breed even when the dogs were not the same dogs he had encountered and even when the situations were entirely different. George's unconscious system had stored some information about a certain type of animal for him. This part of the memory was different from the usual memory, because this memory was not only of actual events, but also of the interpretation of the events.

George's mind's interpretation was that all German Shepherds were inherently dangerous. If you were bitten by a dog twice in your life and both times that dog was a German Shepherd, the interpretation the mind makes may be that German Shepherds as a breed are dangerous and may bite you. This special condition of George's memory storage unit is what is called "generalization" in psychology.

Let's think about the impressions stored in George's memory. First, there is the impression of the actual biting incident. He was arguing with his wife, feeling very emotional, and while in that state, he was bitten by a dog. Later, when the same emotions were provoked, he felt pain in his leg in the same area where he was bitten. The emotional triggers had tied him into the pain of the incident.

Secondly, George had stored in his memory an interpretation based on his experiences with German Shepherds. This interpretation was that all such dogs were dangerous. What do you suppose will happen when George encounters German Shepherds in the future? George has many impressions stored, and his memory can recall and interpret many of them at any given moment.

George may find someday that the sight of a German Shepherd may initiate a response which he does not understand. It may be emotional or it may be physical, but *there will be some type of "irrational" or inexplicable response.* He may find that he has some discomfort at the site of the bite. He may find that he becomes irritated with his wife for no apparent reason. The responses will generally be so small that he may not notice them. In George's case, the end result of all of these impression connections may not be dangerous or troublesome to him.

George's story is a simple example of impressions which can cause some physical and mental responses. George was able to understand the reasons for his responses with an explanation of the process of impression storage, but for many people, the explanation is not so easy.

THE STRESS OF SUCCESS

Tom had not only the responsibility of a vice-presidency of a university, but also the personal responsibility for three children. His divorce left him with the full care of the children, and he had become an expert on balancing his time during the first few months following his divorce.

Tensions from the property settlement, from his wife's abrupt end to their "happy" marriage, and from his children's adolescent rebellion mounted within Tom to a climax point when he found himself uncontrollably depressed. Tom had always been admired for his "take charge" attitude and the President of the university depended on him. Tom had never let anyone down . . . until now.

Tom began to spend most of his day at work just trying to organize his thoughts. He found that he could not remember the simplest things. He found that his skills of managing his large staff were "dull." Tom felt that his days were just drifting by and he had no control over either their content or their outcome. In short, Tom was a mess. He was a disaster looking for somewhere to happen. On the surface, Tom seemed fine. But, you see, Tom was an expert at hiding his true emotions.

Tom did not identify his condition as depression. As a matter of fact, Tom did not identify any emotions very well. All of Tom's life he had carefully and powerfully taken charge of every aspect of his life, professionally and privately. He had accomplished all of the goals he had set out to achieve. He had the children he always wanted and the suburban dream house complete with pool. Tom was well respected in his work and had risen to the top with what seemed like little effort.

All of that appeared to be crumbling before him, and he felt powerless for the first time ever. Tom came to one of our seminars. He had no idea of the changes he would experience because of that seminar. He knew he had to do something because at that time only he knew his skills were slipping away. He had to do something before everyone else found out.

Tom listened as we talked about the importance of impressions from past experiences on our present lives. He listened as we discussed with others the impact of stress on their lives. Others in the group shared some experiences that Tom never imagined some of these people could have had. He knew some of the men and women in the room strictly by their reputations. Top level administrators do not easily share their weaknesses, especially among their peers, *but these people were not sharing weaknesses.* All of them were sharing experiences in which they had been pushed up against some wall. The experiences challenged them to find solutions. They talked about their "personal best" and were sure that if they had not had any challenges, they could not have achieved what they had.

Tom listened intently and became intrigued with the idea that stress, first of all, was a common experience, and secondly, could have advantages. Tom had never really identified his forgetfulness, "dullness," or his other depression symptoms as stress. He of course had said on several occasions that he was "stressed out" and irritable with the children or his staff. It was funny that he considered the two situations so similar. The staff were like his children. He felt responsible for them but he also felt that they should "obey." Tom had always called the shots at home or at work. Obedience was always an important concept to Tom and he was about to learn why.

Tom asked to be placed on the list for our Executive Stress Program. He wanted to know more about stress and just how he could use it, not to overcome his depression, but to become stronger. In a few weeks after the seminar, Tom started his program. Tom's reaction to the stress of his divorce had triggered impressions which were buried deep within his memory. He had erected barriers to feelings from childhood to protect himself from the pains of his extremely unhappy life.

Tom had no reason to think about his childhood experiences until now because he always felt that he had risen above those experiences; he had imposed a new lifestyle which would never allow for failure. Tom's father had never accepted anything less than complete obedience from Tom and his brothers and sisters. His word was law and Tom obeyed no matter what. In order to be obedient, Tom had learned to become an automaton who went on his way doing the "right thing" without question. The barriers Tom built to protect himself from his father's wrath were strong. The barriers were so strong that Tom himself could not break them down.

THE PRIME DIRECTIVE USES MEMORY

The energy system's "prime directive" protects us from danger and pain. If we think of the brain as a computer, the programs we install into our computers manage the output of the system. The prime directive uses these programs to direct all of our functions and thoughts so that we have control.

Tom's computer had been programmed to shut down at the first sign of failure. The divorce obviously was viewed as a failure. After he knew that he could not control the situation and that divorce was inevitable, his system drew on its prime directive for protection and shut down the emotional releases which Tom really needed. He had become almost paralyzed by the shift in his energy.

Too much energy was being used to repress these childhood "energy programs" brought on by failure. Tom was actually starved for energy to make decisions and to manage his life. His children became the symbols of his own childhood, and when his children tried to rebel, Tom felt his own repressed rebellion from childhood rearing its head. Tom's program kicked in, and he viewed that rebellion as completely unacceptable. He tried to impose obedience on his children just as it had been imposed upon him. But, there was something going on within Tom which caused him to shut down. The cycle continued and Tom became immobilized by the system which was desperately trying to protect him, but was actually impairing his judgment. Tom went through a series of sessions in which he recalled the experiences with his father which caused him to shut down as a child. From the adult perspective, Tom could see that the child had no power over the adult father. The two feelings were so closely associated in Tom's memory that the withdrawal from emotion caused him to become like the adult in his memory. He became overcontrolling with the children and anyone else around him.

It was Tom's old impressions which caused him to react in such a way, but it was his imbalanced energy system which caused Tom's stress. Without the stress, Tom would never have developed the stress response symptoms which were eventually going to help him to find balance in his life again emotionally. The release of his emotional energy was a powerful force to help Tom gain a self-awareness and self-confidence that was truly a part of him and not just a facade.

THE NEEDLE IN THE HAYSTACK

What happens if the impressions involved are more dramatic and life-threatening? What if the impressions involve a more traumatic incident and one which can be extremely painful or emotional? The impressions stored every second of every day come from all of our experiences. The experiences may be pleasant or, for some, viciously unpleasant. Depending upon the type of impressions stored, the emotional or physical intensity of the responses will be either minor or major.

Let's consider another scenario about the impact of impressions on a person's energy system. Let's imagine something very unpleasant and violent.

98

Kelly was walking home late one night after a long hard day at the office. She was a personnel manager with many, many "personnel" problems. The pressure of her position with the company was at times almost unbearable. She was very young and there were some in the company who did not feel she deserved the position she held. There were others who had been with the company longer and who "deserved" the job. Nevertheless, she was in the position and was making the best of it.

She lived very close to the office and often walked home to clear her head from the day's activities. She wanted to walk this night because she had a date, and she wanted to be able to "leave the office behind" for the evening. As she walked, she was thinking about the day and the problems she had. She thought about the men who resented her and about the women who were jealous of her. But, she felt she was doing a good job, and she was proud of her accomplishments.

She was looking forward to her date because the fellow she was meeting was new in her life. He was a handsome man with a quick intellect and a good sense of humor. She had known him only a short time, but she felt that perhaps they could develop a close relationship over time. She was thinking about the conversations they may have that evening and about the possible future with this man.

There was hope in her future and she was feeling a great deal better the closer she came to her doorstep. The evening was very warm, and she enjoyed listening to the trees blowing in the light breeze. She heard the sounds of other people in their apartments preparing dinner, talking among themselves, and generally, having a good time.

As she came out of the shadows of a large elm tree, she sensed that there was someone behind her. She could not see anyone, but she "knew" someone was there. The street was just dark enough that shadows obstructed her view. She quickened her pace and continued toward her door.

Suddenly, she felt herself being pulled from behind and she knew in an instant, she was in trouble. Before she could scream, her attacker covered her mouth and dragged her into the alley beside her apartment building. The assault was over in a matter of minutes. Kelly's attacker fled and she found herself lying alone in the dark.

Now, let's talk about impressions. How many memory "pictures" can you count in this story? There are literally thousands of little pieces of physical, emotional, and mental impressions stored over a period of perhaps 15 to 20 minutes of clock time. Kelly's energy system has collected and stored sights, sounds, feelings, sensations, thoughts, and interpretations in what was a very traumatic evening.

Do you recall stories of people who were involved in similar situations in real life or from movies and television programs? Have you read newspaper accounts of persons involved in similar incidents? Or, do you have personal knowledge of such a violent encounter? In any event, do you truly realize how much the impact of such a relatively short incident has on the human energy storage system?

THE POWER OF IMPRESSIONS

If every 27th of a second an impression is stored in the memory, there are literally thousands of impressions involved in the incident just described. Unfortunately, the event is so devastating to the victim, that the effect of the incident continues long after the actual occurrence. When the memory of that event is recalled, all of the experience is available for recall. But, does the victim remember all of the event in detail? If he or she did, it would be like reliving the incident just as it happened! The victim would recall every nuance of emotion from fear to anger to terror to helplessness to any other of the possible reactions he or she might have had.

When the victim is made to recall the event, the entire storage unit is accessed, but does the victim's internal protective defense system allow this to happen? Perhaps not. The prime directive, remember, is to protect and defend the entire system or the individual. The prime directive in the energy system will do everything in its power to defend the system from harm. Reliving violent and painful events can do harm. The system will not allow the entire event to be recalled at one time. To do so would perhaps be too much for the person to handle.

What happens then? The system stores the information in separate "compartments" of the memory so that the information cannot be accessed at one time. The same principle is found in computer programming. The computer data is stored in various ways so that the information is protected. The access to any part of the file is limited based on the kinds of commands we give the computer. The human memory storage system is just the same. The system stores information in such a way as to protect itself from an overload of information at one time.

In the case of Kelly, she did not handle the attack well at all and in future months became very depressed. Eventually, she had to take a leave of absence from her job and find ways with which to deal with her fears, angers, and her emotional responses.

Kelly had no visual memory of the man to recall for the police investigators. She told them that it was so dark she had not seen the attacker's face. She could not identify the attacker even if they caught him. She felt many emotions and wanted only to forget the whole thing and go on with her life.

Kelly had many of the typical reactions of persons who have been involved in such incidents. She had nightmares and she was often afraid to venture out at night. She never walked in her neighborhood alone. She hid away in her apartment and tried to forget.

The new romance suffered because she was so emotionally distraught she could not have any relaxation time. She certainly could not forget what had happened long enough to have any kind of enjoyment. She was sinking further and further into the depths of her own fears. She desperately needed help. She was eventually led to the help of a specialist who dealt with rape and other forms of violent assaults. The counselor wanted to help Kelly and others like her by having Kelly face the incident and explore the reasons why she was carrying the emotions with her for so long. The counselor knew that Kelly had to get on with her life in some way; otherwise, the attacker would have won twice . . . first, by destroying Kelly's confidence and secondly, by destroying her future.

The rape counselor tried many types of approaches which were unsuccessful with Kelly. The minute that the event was discussed in any way, Kelly became inconsolable and could not continue with the session. The counselor wanted to try a form of recall therapy in which Kelly could actually relive the incident and "purge" the memory of it.

In fact, the counselor was attempting to bring all of the emotions to the surface so that Kelly could understand her reactions and change them for the better. The theory was good; the reality was not. Kelly began the session recalling the incident with the counselor's help. The counselor had read the police files and had some information about the incident that Kelly herself did not. The counselor "filled in the gaps" where Kelly had forgotten and helped Kelly remember.

Kelly remembered. *Kelly remembered.* She brought all of the information about the incident into the open and into her conscious recall. *Kelly remembered.* She could *hear* the trees blowing in the wind. She could *hear* the voices of her neighbors. Kelly remembered. She could *"feel"* the attacker behind her in the darkness. *Kelly remembered.* She felt the pain of the attack. She felt the damp concrete under her back. She remembered the fear she had that she would be killed. Kelly remembered. Not only did she remember the physical sensations, she remembered the emotional feelings. Kelly remembered the entire experience just as if it were happening all over again.

When all of that memory came to Kelly, all of the impressions she had stored in that 15 to 20 minutes of her life were recalled in one large unit. The attack only took a small portion of the 15 or 20 minute walk, but the impressions of the time were collected together and recalled together. Not only did she remember the attack, she remembered the pleasant thoughts she had. She recalled the thoughts about her co-workers and the problems she had at work.

Kelly collapsed under the weight of the memory because it was not controlled. She had lost the control of the energy system because she asked too much. She could not sort through the information and decide which pieces she wanted to recall. She got the whole package dumped in her lap, so to speak. She was in an overload situation just like a computer, and she "burned out her circuits." She emotionally collapsed and was reduced to a terrified, unbalanced collection of memories.

CONTROLLING THE MEMORY

Why does this happen? The system will retrieve what we ask of it. Because she was asked to recall the incident, she did. She reached into the memory of the experience and asked for it all. If you would ask your computer to give you all of the data stored within its memory at one time, your computer would be "stressed" and would, no doubt, not cooperate. By asking for everything without any limits, the system collapses. Kelly's system collapsed in much the same way.

If these impressions are stored in several different areas, why not retrieve them as they are stored? We can retrieve them one piece at a time. If we retrieve one piece at a time, the individual can explore only one piece at a time and learn from that one piece. The energy system will provide one part of the impression stored rather than the entire incident which may be a collection of hundreds of impressions. Many of them may be extremely traumatic.

It has been our experience with clients who have suffered some physical, emotional, or mental trauma that by taking only one piece of the entire event at one time the client does not collapse. In cases of abuse situations when there are many, many events which occur over a period of time, the victim has stored hundreds of impressions. The impressions collect as each event occurs adding to the total package of memory. In these cases, to recall the entire abuse situation is desperately painful. The victim reacts, perhaps, by repressing the memory of some of the events in order to survive. This technique is part of the defense mechanism for the energy system. The repression does protect the person for a while, but eventually the repression cannot hold in the torrent of emotional reactions such incidents create. At some point, the person must deal with the abuse or detach in some way.

By using the energy system to explore the events of the experience and by taking only one piece at a time, the person does not run the risk of "re-energizing" the impressions. In other words, in the case of Kelly, by reliving every nuance of the event in therapy, she may have formed new impressions over the ones already in place. These new impressions could well be even more damaging to her in the future. If not handled properly, she could slip further and further into the depression she is seeking to resolve. The weight of all of the impressions could be too much for her.

The story of Kelly and the attack is all too common in this period of violence in which we all live. Kelly's story illustrates an important part of understanding the ways in which we can use the energy system to our advantage. We do not need to experience the horrible incident of physical attack or physical abuse in order to suffer from some of the same symptoms as Kelly.

Someone once said that most of us live lives of "quiet desperation." We do not all have violence visited upon us even though the news reports could make us wonder. We live in a society fraught with dangers and possibilities that our grandparents never imagined. The social pressures, the economic hardships, and the criminal realities with which we are all faced sometimes seem unbearably near to home. We are not here to solve those realities or address them. The story of Kelly, who is an imaginary victim, is used here to make a point about impressions and the ways in which those impressions can be used positively or negatively. We feel that the positive use of those impressions is found in Energy Dynamics[R]. Through the use of Energy Dynamics[R], anyone can access the right information in the right way to turn what could be a very negative response into a positive one.

We do not all have such dramatic incidents with which to deal, but we all do have millions of impressions with which to learn every day. The impressions are there for us to use in the most positive way possible. As we discussed earlier, we do not think of incidents or memories to be either negative or positive in and of themselves. The *use* of those memories and experiences is either positive or negative for us. What we call the "positive stress factor" is the use of those impressions to alter our reactions and to improve our lives.

A LITTLE GIRL'S MEMORY

My father was dead. My mother said that he had gone to Heaven and that he was happy. We would have to learn to get along without him. It was the day after Christmas. I had given him some new slipper socks on Christmas Eve. We were at the farm that day. Now, we were in my grandmother's bedroom full of shadows and the strange sound of city traffic. I was five years old. *I didn't want my father to go to Heaven.*

At that moment and in the years that followed, the "five-year-old" within me relentlessly hung on to that final moment with her father and the possibilities that might have been. The "five-year-old" split from the adult who was Mary Lee. She moved into an isolated cocoon of sadness and, mostly, anger. That part of me became my greatest source of power and motivation in my life. The energy of my anger pushed me to succeed and achieve.

My father, John Lee Webb, was well-liked in the small farm community in which we lived. He was an entrepreneur and businessman even though, at the time, I didn't know that. He didn't even know that. He was just making a living for his family. He had a wonderful sense of humor and enjoyed a good time. He and my mother had developed a good and loving relationship and worked hard together. My father always wanted children. When I finally arrived after they had been married for many years, I was "Daddy's girl." I was secure in both his and my mother's love. My father did what most men of his generation did not do. He was directly involved in my care along with my mother.

As I grew, he taught me what he thought of as good human values . . . sharing, respecting other people's property, and telling the truth. He helped me to understand that there were consequences to my actions and that sometimes people were hurt by what we said. He introduced me to the beauty of nature and at the same time, taught me respect for all living things. I often wonder if my interest in the wonder of the human energy system as part of a greater universe started at that young age at my father's knee.

Most of all, my father taught me self-responsibility. Being on a farm was a dangerous place for a toddler, and I learned some hard lessons about what I could and could not do. An old impression of those days still lives on that farm in Idaho. My father's old combine still stands on the fields he farmed. One day, when I was about two or three, I thought it would be fun to climb up on that huge combine and kick dirt and chaff down on the hired hand. My dad told me to stop, but I continued. He then told the hired man that if I persisted, he had my father's permission to discipline me. He was teaching me that there are consequences to every action we take. A few years ago, as I walked those fields, I looked at that old combine and remembered.

When my father died, I tried to be strong in a way that every little girl thinks that her father would be strong. The strength of the five-year-old and the ambition to be all that her father would have wanted her to be were powerful forces.

Many positive things came out of the tragedy of his death at such a young age. Many changes in our lifestyle occurred. We moved from the country to the city. My mother had to assume the roles of father and mother and by moving into the city with me, she opened a new world to the little girl. A world of culture and

106

education was opened to me. With all of the positive outcomes of this event in my young life, there were also impressions of anger and grief which I would carry with me for the next 35 years. It wasn't until I started my own stress program with Energy Dynamics^R that I fully faced those impressions of emotion stored within me.

Periodically the anger I felt, mixed with the great sadness, erupted like a volcano. I had been abandoned by my father, and the fear of abandonment had lain like a sleeping giant within me, often intruding into my relationships with other people. My profession was based on helping people find their own strength, but my strength came from an anger out of control.

During one of my sessions, the impression I remembered was the scene in which my mother had told me that Dad had died. The five-year-old had attached an image to the words as only a five-year-old could. My mother's words were: "He has gone to Heaven and is happy now. We will have to learn to get along without him." The five-year-old's image was of a coffin suspended half way between Heaven and earth. The coffin had a tether line attached to it, and the five-year-old held on to the other end of the line. I saw myself as the five-year-old with pigtails clutching the tether.

The five-year-old child did not want her dad to go away so she was hanging on. The last tangible connection she had to her dead father was the coffin. If she could hold on to it, he would not be gone forever. The little girl could not possibly understand the event, so her only recourse was to "hold on." And she did. The five-year-old held on to that coffin for years. As a child of five, Mary Lee had no power to control the event, so she created the power in her image. As an adult, I could let go of the tether because I could assure that five-year-old who still lived inside me that I could take care of her. I had the power.

As the little girl let go of the tether, the coffin drifted away. The anger went with it. There are those who say I am easier to live with now! I am no longer split between the defenseless child and the powerful adult. I am still my father's daughter, but I am also a woman directing my own life.

"We are not interested in the possibilities of defeat"

Queen Victoria

SEVEN

THE POWER OF SELF-ESTEEM

My mother drives a sports car. *A red sports car.* She is also on the sunny side of 75 years old. If she ever dreamed that her age would be the subject of public discussion, she would have disowned her daughter, Rebecca, long ago. My mother belongs here in the chapter on self-esteem and empowerment for many reasons, none of which a daughter ever imagines. As a career mother and wife, my mother is not the typical liberated, empowered superwoman of the 1990's about whom we all read. As a matter of fact, her power came rather late in life. That is precisely why we want to tell you about her.

INDEPENDENCE AND POWER

Helen always lived her life under the shadow of family, society, and obligation. Her whole life was wrapped up in her family and duty. For many years, the center of her life was in her own mother's home. She made the pilgrimages to the family home every week without fail. There was never any question that she would not show up. *It was expected.* This was the world as she knew it. There was a "self-core" like a spark of independence firing somewhere deep within her giving her strength and a quiet dignity that some never saw or understood.

Life moved along for Helen with ups and downs, hopes and disappointments, comedies and tragedies. The years slipped by too quickly and Helen was soon visited by her husband's serious illness. As many women of her generation, her husband's illness and eventual death was an expected reality. Many women are the caretakers of ill husbands and the survivors of their husbands' deaths. Many women live out the rest of their lives in a kind of limbo caused by the separation from their mates. When she was married almost 50 years ago, one married for life, for better or worse.

With my father's long hospitalization, I watched Helen change subtly, but dramatically. At one point, about a week before his death, she turned to me and asked, "Is your father going to die?" I said, "Yes." She was very quiet. I did not know exactly what she was thinking. After a short period of time, she turned to me and said, "Where are we going to take him?" I hesitated because I did not quite know what she meant. I thought perhaps she was in a state of denial about the impending death. She went on. "Which funeral home should we take him to?" I found myself smiling deep inside me because, for probably the first time in my life, my mother was showing a new sense of independence by taking charge of a difficult situation. She had taken hold the situation, evaluated it, gathered the necessary information, and had begun the process of making a decision. A woman who grew up in a world which demanded routine and expectations was now about to take charge of her life.

She surprised us a great deal during that time and I often caught myself looking at her with the shocked realization that she was my mother. She seemed so different to me.

The woman who had looked to everyone for support in the past now had to support other people. She had to find strength somewhere to carry herself through the days and months of stress ahead of her. After her husband's death, Helen was faced with a new reality. How was she going to live alone after all of these years?

My mother's "life after death" is the cornerstone of the empowerment which can come from stress. The positive use of her stress came from the way in which, at an age when some people are

109

preparing for their own deaths, Helen started her new life. At the age of 72, she began an odyssey of discovery and independence. She now travels, knits, shops, laughs, and looks for the next adventure *just around the corner.* Ethel Barrymore once said "You grow up the day you have the first real laugh - at yourself."

Those who know Helen marvel at her resilient nature and her sense of humor. She faced stress and pressure so intense that some would have collapsed. *She did not.* The miracle of the human energy system and its power to achieve self-esteem is the ability to change and grow no matter what the age. You will never catch us looking at someone older and saying, "Don't bother. People don't change at that age."

They do. The wealth of the human energy system is found in this ability to change and grow each day in different ways. Helen is an inspiration to me and as her daughter, I am very fortunate to call her mother and friend. She has taught me about self-esteem and self-worth. She is living a life of empowerment by learning from her stress. She looks at the world with a positive eye toward a future she wants to explore.

SELF-ESTEEM AND EMPOWERMENT

"Self-esteem" is a term which is thrown around a great deal these days as people try to find their own self-worth. What is self-esteem? We all know what the word, "self", means, but what does "esteem" mean? If we look in our dictionaries, we find that "esteem" has many meanings. "Respect", "assurance," "confidence," "presence," "value," and "love" are all listed as possible meanings for the word "esteem." When we combine that word with "self" we have a clue as to why so many have a problem with their self-esteem.

If we hold others in "esteem," we admire and value them. We respect them. We are usually assured that those persons are worth something. We have confidence in their "presence." We care about them and honor them. How many of us have the same feelings about ourselves? Do you consciously honor yourself?

Do you respect your accomplishments . . . or your failures? Do you value your place in life as worthy of admiration and love? If you do, you are the leader about whom we have been talking. An achiever or leader in whatever field is someone who has self-esteem and exhibits all of the feelings about himself or herself we have just listed. The old cliche says that "you cannot love another if you do not love yourself."

BALANCING ACHIEVEMENTS

Jackie had always been an achiever. Her love of other people and her gift for conversation were perfect qualities needed in her position as a sales director for a major company. A newly formed publishing firm had hired some of the brightest young people in the country to manage the company. Jackie was among these ambitious, enthusiastic, and creative people.

She is an example of what Faith Popcorn, in her book THE POPCORN REPORT, calls the "Acceleration Syndrome." Ms. Popcorn describes this syndrome as "the speeding up of everyone's life to a breakneck pace." (Popcorn, page 191). Jackie was challenged by her new position. She was the type of director any CEO would want on the team. Jackie used much of her energy enjoying life outside the office, too. People enjoyed her and as a result, she had many friends. Jackie was always entertaining and networking with business groups. Jackie loved life. Her self-esteem was constantly being stroked by those she knew.

She loved people and tried to help them whenever and however she could. Because she was such a good listener, many came to Jackie to ask advice. Many leaned on her for support and help with problems. She set few limits with her friends and often spent long hours solving other people's problems. The long hours took their toll beginning one beautiful spring day.

Jackie always had some minor illnesses, and she rarely slowed down long enough to attend to them. Her body was sending her stress signals which she had ignored for weeks. Jackie could barely crawl from her apartment to her morning staff meeting. Her office assistant urged her to go home and rest, *but Jackie had too much to do.* Her self-esteem grew from her job and her personal life. It did not come from a core within her which responded to the signal to slow down. Jackie wanted to keep going and she did. Until, she could no longer.

Her doctor diagnosed "Chronic Fatigue Syndrome" and Jackie was told to rest, slow down her professional obligations, and take care of herself. Jackie had caused this condition to develop and become worse, not because she didn't care, but because she did not take the signals seriously. She was faced with the knowledge now that the answers to her recovery were to be found within her. She recognized that the same signal of stress and physical strain which forced her to stop her frantic pace of life was also the signal for a renewal. Her lifestyle choices would have to be altered. She had to redefine her self-worth by paying attention to her own system.

Jackie began the Executive Dynamics Program by taking a long look at her diet. The cocktails and the coffee pick-me-ups had to go. She started to eat more balanced meals at more appropriate times of the day. She started to be more aware of her physical body. The aches and pains which she had soothed with medication were really signals to her that she needed exercise and an occasional therapeutic massage.

The most important lesson Jackie learned was to prioritize her life. In order to do that, she had to face the reality that all of the things she did for other people, she had to start doing for herself first. Her self-esteem crisis had led her to understand the true power of being a good friend and employee. It did not come from the love of others. It came from her love of herself. By learning to accept and love herself, Jackie listened more carefully to the needs of her own body. She was no longer ignoring the signals. She was learning from them.

SELF-ESTEEM COMES FROM KNOWLEDGE

There are many of our clients who have faced this dilemma head on and who have discovered more depth within them than they ever imagined. The discovery of self-esteem does not come from merely analyzing the conditions of your life. Stephen R. Covey explains in THE 7 HABITS OF HIGHLY EFFECTIVE PEOPLE that "our self-esteem empowers us to examine our own thoughts." (Covey, page 130). Self-esteem grows from the knowledge, the interpretations, and the acceptance of who and what you are.

Remember that the energy system stores all of the impressions of your life for use whenever and however you wish. It is truly up to you to use what is stored in a positive way. No one can teach you a simple solution to achieving self-esteem. There are no teachers alive today or in the past who have any more power than you to develop your self-esteem.

From the beginning of her life, Marie has somehow always found her own way. The family story goes that at the age of two, she crawled up the stairs and lay claim to an upstairs bedroom for her own. She walked four miles to high school to practice for the girls' basketball team. After college she started a teaching career in a rural school, met her husband, and became a rancher.

The Great Depression and a world war made life challenging for Marie and her husband. Through it all she had developed the steely determination which would later help her to survive the tragic death of her young husband. After his death, she took control and the responsibility of being a young single mother raising a child alone. Her sense of self-esteem and empowerment came later.

Marie, even with all of her determination, could not prevent life from taking its turns and twists of fate. Her mother needed care and she took the responsibility as she always had in her life. Sometimes her sense of personal independence collided with her duties to her mother, but she was not a woman to shirk her obligations. She stood by her mother until, with that same determined dignity that Marie had inherited, the 96 year old matriarch died.

A short time later, Marie cared for her brother who was dying of cancer with the same sense of responsibility. After his death, Marie was alone for really the first time in her life. What now? There was no one to care for but herself. She faced what everyone faces at some point in life. Her story is different than some.

Remember, we're talking about the power that comes from stress and adversity. Marie faced the death of a husband, mother, and brother. Not an unusual set of circumstances, but definitely a series which was to change her view of her life. The security of having a 96 year old mother would give anyone the idea that mortality was not an imminent reality. She basked in her own mother's presence for 70 years. With her mother gone, Marie started to look at herself as her own person.

Carl Jung described the self "as the emergence of an integrative center within the personality and the fruit of the individuation process." When a person starts to know herself or himself as a real person, then the power of the individual emerges. *And did it emerge.*

Marie took to the road, literally. She traveled. She volunteered her time at her church. She developed new friendships and relationships. She emerged from duty into choice. She became an empowered woman. She had always been a determined woman, but now there was this new center within her which Gloria Steinem calls a "revolution within" to self-esteem.

Mark Twain probably said it best. "It's a good idea to obey all the rules when you are young just so you'll have the strength to break them when you're old."

I am proud to be Marie's daughter, Mary Lee, and every day I find new reasons to be proud of my mother's accomplishments. She has shown me how a sense of duty can carry you through some very tough times. Blended with a sense of one's own power and self-worth a certain depth of wisdom and gentleness evolves. This makes the involvement with other people so much more satisfying.

114

My mother, Marie Webb, is an inspiration to me. I hope I can be one to her.

EM"POWER"MENT COMES FROM WITHIN

"Self-empowerment" is also a catch word of the 1990's. Empowerment itself is a word which conjures up different meanings to different people. One of our friends was concerned about the word; he felt that the word needed an object. In other words, if you were empowered, you had to be empowered to do "something." To many people the word means that you are giving power to someone else. The implication is that the other person is unable to do that for himself or herself. In Energy Dynamics^R, empowerment means "achieving self-esteem." Empowerment is the ability to entrust, to enable, and to validate.

Sometimes, we don't believe that we ourselves are empowered. We sometimes are shocked to discover that we are capable, trustworthy, and validated. There is a wonderful story about Pope John XXIII. He reportedly said, "It often happens that I wake at night and begin to think about a serious problem and decide I must tell the Pope about it. Then I wake up completely and remember that I am the Pope."

If we empower ourselves, we do not do that at the expense of someone else. There is no threat with true empowerment because if you develop or achieve self-esteem, you do not have to take anything from anyone else. You are a person who can trust yourself to make decisions about your life. You can know that no decision you make will harm another person.

Likewise, no decision another person makes can harm you if you have achieved self-esteem. The whole concept of self-esteem is one which takes many twists, turns, and detours in our lives. It is an adventure for some of us. For others, it is a misadventure and, sometimes, a disaster. The disturbing truth about cult activities and mind control groups is that those with low or no self-esteem are ready targets for control. Without a true sense of who and what you are and a trust that you can make decisions on your own, you can be made to believe anything.

One of the most important elements of our seminars in Energy Dynamics^R is the lesson that whatever you learn, you must *make it your own* before you can use it. We are all individuals. We must all find our own truths. Just because we espouse a certain viewpoint, it may not fit your individual pattern of thought. You must take it in, interpret it based on your own experience, and then, use it or discount it. *The truth is only the truth for you if you can make it happen.*

We have a good friend who has a marvelous way of analyzing everything she hears. When she analyzes, she often overanalyzes. As a matter of fact, she has tried to break herself of the habit of analyzing too much. She tells us that before she spends too much time thinking about some decision she analyzes the subject to decide *whether it merits any analysis!!* Do you imagine that she would be a pushover for mind control? Not on your life! She has discovered her own way of making decisions. She has reached a level of self-esteem which allows her to trust herself to make decisions.

THE SEARCH FOR POWER

The development of self-esteem in anyone is a long, active process. You have to work on it. Some of our clients over the years have faced challenges which caused them to change lifestyles, partners, and careers. They have had to change their own visions of themselves. We have a fantastic capacity for change and it is the development of self-esteem which allows us to change well.

Bill had been a personnel director for almost twenty-five years when he realized that everything for which he had worked all those years had been for other people and not himself. Bill had become expert in communicating with his staff and adept at blending diverse groups of people into working teams.

All through the years of successful management, Bill had only experienced success in his profession, not in his personal life. Bill knew that the manager who is successful on only one front of his or her life cannot continue to fool himself or herself or others forever. There is a breaking point for everyone and Bill's breaking point came with a divorce. The children were shocked. The friends were shocked. The co-workers were shocked. *Even Bill's wife of 35 years was shocked.* Bill was amazed that others could not see what was so obvious to him.

He had begun to grow up. He had started to become an individual and he felt the beginnings of self-worth. At the age of 56, Bill started to want more out of life than a successful career and a "perfect" marriage. He wanted to know himself and he wanted to explore the worlds he did not know. This was a mid-life crisis if there ever was one! His children questioned his sanity. His wife questioned his fidelity and his sexual orientation. After all, if he was rejecting her after 35 "happy" years, there must be another woman, or worse, another man.

Bill tried everything to explain, but in the end, he walked away. He walked away from home. He walked away from the town. He walked away from the past. Bill even wanted to get away from "Bill" and referred to himself as "William". He wanted to change everything about himself including his name. His explained that he didn't feel like "Bill" anymore. He wanted a new life and a new name to go with it.

This was just the beginning. He took a leave of absence from his job, bought a new car, and set off on an odyssey of discovery from one end of the country to the other. He wanted to find himself. He had been working hard through the sixties and missed being a "hippie." He wanted to try it, he said.

William's journey of discovery took many turns and twists before he finally learned the reason for his search. William had never had the chance to be William or Bill. He was always the reflection of what everyone expected. Bill had been the model manager, the model husband, and the model father for a full generation. There was more to Bill than people knew. He was an innovator without an avenue for innovation. He was a creator without a mission for creation. He was searching for something lost in the past. The past had not been kind to Bill because he was never allowed to grow up. He never explored the horizons and never even knew there were horizons until he learned about his energy system. The energy system within Bill was something when unleashed led him into new territory. He found that he was empowered all along, but never knew it.

He could do anything he wanted. He just didn't know what that was. He had tapped into the power, but he didn't know how to use it. He had never been the director of his own life. With that directorship in hand, he looked for ways to use it. Like a kid with a new toy, William tried everything. When he tired of one toy, he picked up another.

The important thing about William is that without the knowledge of his own powerbase in energy, Bill would never emerge into himself. He started to like himself and to recognize his own strengths without being told what to think, say, or feel. As a result of his own strength, he frightened those who knew the old Bill. They felt uncomfortable with this new model who didn't act or sound like Bill. When we change, others are sometimes uncomfortable because they have certain expectations of how we should act. If we change, they must accommodate. Most people don't know how to accommodate to change.

William struggled with many in his past life, but eventually he reached a stage when he did know what he wanted and who he was. He was no longer frightened and he was no longer frightening to those around him. They all sensed that Bill was not gone. He was just a new, improved model.

William is a good friend, a good ex-husband, and a good man because he is now truly his own person.

"No bird soars too high if he soars with his own wings."

William Blake

Think Bite #8

You are a constantly changing energy system using your stress to give you the power to make those changes. One of the best pieces of advice given us over the years was by Marcel Vogel. During a particularly stressful period for Rebecca, he advised her to start a journal. She looked at him, blinked, and said, "I don't have time to write. Besides, what good would that do? I need answers." Of course, that was his point. The answers could be found by keeping a journal of her thoughts and feelings.

Many of us keep diaries or we have in the past. The secrets we wrote to "Dear Diary" were usually about dreams, hopes, desires, and wishes. We kept them locked away and hidden from others' views because we weren't sure that we had the right to have those dreams or thoughts. We glimpsed our self-awareness but really didn't feel confident enough to voice it publicly.

Well, some of us still don't. The only really important person you have to tell is yourself. *So, tell yourself.* You may find as Rebecca did that the answers were there within her and that by writing them, she could make them realities.

Here's the advice. Buy a notebook. Every day or evening at about the same time, take out your notebook and write. Some of us have a great deal of difficulty writing without purpose, so we will give you a purpose. Put the date on the page. Under the date write these phrases. "I am . ," "I want . ,"   "I will . ." Then, just fill in the blanks. You may find just one word to fit the blank that day. Or you may find torrents of thoughts to write. Whatever you do, only fill one page. Sometimes, that page will be almost empty. Some other days, the page will be filled to overflowing. It doesn't matter. *Just do it.*

Skip a page in the notebook. The next day, write on the next page. Date. "I am . ." "I want . ." "I will . ."

Now, the best part. After about two weeks begin to go back two weeks in the notebook and read the entries. After you read what you had written, use the next page, the one you left blank the first time around, to comment on what you just read. Write your ideas and thoughts about what you wrote two weeks ago.

You can write anything you wish. This is your own journal. It's not for publication unless you become more famous and want to publish it for posterity. In any event, this journal is your energy system journal. Write down your thoughts, your feelings, your ideas for the future, your memories.

Journal writing is a time honored method for keeping your memories, but it can also be so much more. The journal can teach you so much about where you are and where you are going. It can help you understand the stress in your life and it can show you how you are dealing with that stress. Remember that positive change is your goal and the empowering of your own life is the reward.

If you truly want to be successful in using stress positively, start your journal.

THE SEARCH FOR SELF-AWARENESS

As each person meets challenges and changes in his or her own way, the energy style determines the way each person needs to change. In other words, each person processes the experiences of his or her life differently and must change in ways that are complementary to the style. For some energy styles, the use of positive stress comes from a mental change like Bill. He redefined his life from a logical perspective and used his mental acuity to explore new options for himself. He attended classes and traveled the country looking for answers. Sometimes the mental maneuvering was exhausting, but he had gained strength and power from the mental processing.

Sometimes, the stress shows itself emotionally and each person deals with emotional energy in different ways. The road to self-empowerment and self-confidence is very often a road with many roadblocks along the way. Each person uses a different style to break through those blocks to self-awareness and power.

120

Self awareness is not a new concept for Virginia. She has spent an entire lifetime pursuing that elusive "self" about which she had read so much. In the 60's, she participated in sensitivity training groups and encounter groups which were touted as the keys to self-growth and self-esteem. Virginia obtained advanced degrees in counseling and psychology. She studied Native American traditions, bodywork therapies, Gestalt psychotherapy, hypnosis, and family therapy. All of her life she has been a seeker of some truth which seems so difficult to find.

What did she learn from all of this searching for the truth? She learned many things. She developed a respect for many theories which seemed to answer some questions. But, there were still questions for which she had no answers. The answers she found only went so far for her, and she was left feeling that "something" was missing. That missing something was the key to her own self-awareness.

No matter how successful or accomplished she became as a psychologist, there was that missing something which made her do irrational things. She had one great fear. The fear that haunted her from an early age. The fear that she would be left behind. *Abandoned. Rejected.* A fear that most people have to some degree or other. Virginia was a psychologist. She was supposed to have the answers to this problem. She could easily help others with similar problems, but why couldn't she help herself?

It was a disturbing realization that after 20 years of study and exploration in a field which she respected, she found that her field could not provide the answers she needed. Self-esteem was an elusive achievement for Virginia. She could not feel any sense of self-worth because she was always waiting for the abandonment she *KNEW was coming.*

There was a little girl who lived inside Virginia. This little girl was much like other little children who live within adults. There is a popular theme running through psychological circles these days. It is very popular to be identified as an "adult child" of something or other. You can be an "adult child" of an alcoholic. An "adult child" of divorced parents. An "adult child" of codependent parents. There are literally hundreds of support groups centered around this "child within" and there are many theorists who blame many of society's ills on the inability of adults to deal with these "adult children" syndromes.

We know that within us are the memories of our childhoods. It is no mystery that our experiences of youth dictate our adult lives. We are created from our past experiences. In Energy Dynamics[R] we recognize that the experiences of childhood impact on the reactions we have as adults. The power of the childhood memories is seen every day during our seminars and in our private counseling sessions. But, are we to remain ever children? Are we to hold on to those fears, terrors, and impressions throughout our lives? Do you always want to be an "adult child?" Or, do you want to be an integrated adult? Do you want to take from all of your experiences and become the best adult you can be?

Virginia wanted to be the best adult she could be. She wanted to learn from the child within her how to be a strong adult woman with her own power. The psychological theories she had studied were advanced techniques which touched on some of the truths she wanted, but never got to the core of the answer for her. So, her search continued.

Her fear of abandonment sabotaged many of her adult relationships. When she felt closeness develop with anyone professionally or personally, she unconsciously found excuses to break away from the other person. She was a gregarious, fun-loving person who was an instant friend to practically everyone she met. She made people comfortable and she enjoyed most people. Her laugh was infectious and she was extremely successful with her clients. But, when this closeness became too threatening for her, she would drive the person away with her demands or anger. The anger grew from the child within her who was so angry at a father who had abandoned her by dying too soon. She loved her father, and *he had left her behind.* She couldn't be angry with him because . . . well, she loved him. She could be angry with other people!

Whenever there was a stressful situation in any relationship, she drew on her anger and her fear to find the power she lacked in self-esteem. You have to know that Virginia knew what she was doing *intellectually*. She knew the reasons. She understood the theory of the "adult child." After all, she was a psychologist. But, she was an unhappy psychologist.

Virginia never gave much credence to her physical body. She was an athlete who felt well when she was exercising and working out, but other than an occasional ache or pain, she ignored her body. When something happened to it, she went to the doctor. For the most part, she ignored it. She certainly didn't feel that any hard work or emotional stress could impact her physical body! As a matter of fact, her physical body was a scapegoat for her stress. Virginia had a passion for chocolate and coffee. She had discovered early on in her life that when she was depressed or exhausted, a hot fudge sundae or a cup of rich black coffee could lift her up.

Her secretary was often sent on missions of mercy to the local soft ice cream stand just a mile from Virginia's office for her "fix" in between client sessions. The sessions drained her of energy because she was so involved emotionally with her clients. After she felt so drained, the coffee or the sundae lifted her energy level and she felt better.

Day after day she used the caffeine in the chocolate and the coffee as her "pick-me-up." Every day, Virginia's physical body gathered more scars of her abuse. She began to have strange heart palpitations which caused her to panic. She went off to her doctor and walked around for 24 hours with a heart monitor. The physician diagnosed a mitral valve problem and advised some medications for her. As she was leaving his office, he asked the $64,000 question. "Do you drink a lot of coffee?" *Smart physician!*

"Yes," she replied, "All the time." Actually, she didn't tell him about the *amount* of coffee she had been consuming or about the daily "fixes" of chocolate. He threw up his arms and said, "Well, stop it. That just may stop the palpitations." She did and *the heart palpitations stopped, too.*

Another rather interesting thing was happening to Virginia. She was developing some other physical symptoms which were troubling her. One of her good friends told her to consult with Dr. Holmes. Perhaps she needed someone to give her advice about diet and general health. It was that visit which led Virginia to discover that she did have, not just a mind and emotions, but also a physical body for which she was responsible. She could no longer abuse it as if she could trade it in when it malfunctioned. She had to pay attention to the physical symptoms of her stress before those symptoms grew too large.

Well, now wait a minute. We started talking about her emotional difficulty and self-esteem and now, we have her paying attention to her physical body. How could they possibly be connected? It is very simple. We are not just disconnected reflexes, thoughts, and feelings. Where have you read that before? Virginia, like everyone else, is a complex energy system which works as a unit, not in pieces. She is not just a mind without a body. She is not just a body without a mind. She is not just an adult psychologist. She is a blend of the child and the adult. She is a dynamic power plant, changing every day.

Virginia finally found that through blending the physical, mental, and emotional, she could not only control her emotional confusions, but she could actually alter them. She took the stress of her physical symptoms, her emotional outbursts, and her keen intellect and began to build her own power base. Virginia no longer reacted irrationally when faced with any threat. She had a power base now that came from finally accepting the child within her as not just some part that had to be tolerated and handled. She had learned to make that little girl part of the adult Virginia had become.

"To the illumined mind the whole world sparkles with light."

Ralph Waldo Emerson

THE JOURNEY OF DISCOVERY

Self-esteem and self-awareness come after a long journey of discovery. Albert Camus said, "In the depth of winter, I finally learned that within me there lay an invincible summer." The invincible summer is that sense of power which can come from knowing who you are and what you are. The depth of winter can be the stress which causes you to search for answers. Winter's snow covers a promise of spring and summer. The impressions and childhood experiences we all have are like the snow of that winter. Under all of those impressions and experiences lie some fantastic surprises and discoveries.

We're not finished with Virginia. She began to question her own field and profession because she felt that the field had abandoned her own search for the truth. Virginia questioned her profession because it had not helped her with her search. At one point, she wanted to throw it all away and search in new fields for answers. But, Virginia had to know that we are the sum of all we experience. The experiences and vast stores of knowledge she had accumulated over the years were invaluable. She had to learn to take everything she knew and add to it. Nothing we ever experience or learn is a waste of time. We may not always use the things we discover or we may not use them right away or often. But, they are all there to draw upon whenever it is necessary.

Virginia discovered, explored, and devoured knowledge. The result is a woman with power. She is a woman with not only an infectious laugh, but also a happy heart. She is a woman with friends and foes. *A woman alive with possibilities for the future.* A woman named Mary Lee Webb.

FINDING THE KEY TO THE ENERGY SYSTEM

The use of energy by an individual can be more based on physical symptoms than any other aspect. William/Bill dealt with his stress on a mental plane and approached his new life by logically changing his way of living. Virginia/Mary Lee worked into her own power through emotional releases and the understanding that came not from mental logic, but from that intuitive sense that something was "missing. Either way, the end result is what is important. The positive use of any stress can be accomplished through any part of the energy system. Sometimes, the energy style of an individual demands that stress be addressed not emotionally or mentally, but physically first. There are times when a client, because of his or her particular energy style, is more amenable to physical "treatment" and solution than emotional or mental techniques. Many of the highest achievers are those who depend on their physical signals to tell them when they need help. Unfortunately, it is also true of some energy styles that those who are in greatest need of physical attention do not pay attention until the crisis situation exists.

Trying to talk about emotions or logic with someone who is so involved with the physical world is almost impossible. If someone is not comfortable working with emotions, perhaps the physical aspect is the avenue of choice. One particular case comes to mind. Nick is an executive vice-president for a large public relations company. He was anxious on the job and knew that eventually, the stress of continued pressure to succeed would destroy him. He sought out a psychologist even though he had little faith in psychology. He didn't know where else to go.

He had tried prescription medications, long vacations, avoidance, and denial. None worked any better or worse than the others. Finally, with great reluctance, Nick came to Dr. Webb as a client. After about three sessions, he became upset because she kept "after him" to describe his feelings. Imagine. Talking about feelings in front or a stranger. And he didn't like another thing. Dr. Webb laughed a lot! Nick had always believed that feelings were private. That life was serious. Therapists should just tell a person what to do, instead of letting the poor client ramble on searching for a solution.

Nick became so upset that he told Dr. Webb he had enough. This was getting him nowhere. In his last session, Nick complained about his neck hurting because he was sitting at his computer terminal preparing a quarterly report for days. He could hardly concentrate on the session. Half way through the session, Dr. Webb decided that Nick needed more physical care right now than emotional so she asked one of the muscular therapists on staff in the clinic if she had time to see Nick.

Nick had his first therapeutic muscle massage work done that day. He had always been leery of body therapies and had even made jokes about massage parlors and masseurs. But, here he was with a physical pain that was preventing him from thinking. *This could not be tolerated.* He submitted to the therapy.

That started a series of sessions in which Nick finally began to work through some of his stress. By working first with his body and the physical symptoms, Nick was able to bypass the overt discussion of emotions. Nick was able to talk with the therapist during the sessions about what he was feeling physically easier than what was going on emotionally. But through these sessions, he found that even the therapist had similar stress on her job. Nick even discovered that they had something else in common. They shared similar childhoods and similar problems relating to others about feelings and emotions.

Nick was able to get control of his entire energy system by starting in the area which was the least threatening to him.

Often when we begin to turn stress into positive power, we identify that a person must approach the stress from the energy style he or she exhibits and not from the perspective of the coach.

SOMETIMES KNOWLEDGE IS NOT ENOUGH

Winston is 35 years old and he has crippling arthritis. This is his story.

Winston came to Dr. Holmes a few years ago under the threat of surgery to replace his knees because of the progression of his arthritic condition. He was being told by experts in arthritis that there were no alternatives to his condition and that surgery was absolutely necessary.

Winston was very frightened of any new therapy, but he was more frightened of the surgery and the possible disability resulting from that. He started his therapy by changing his diet and trying to cut back on the foods which are known to contribute to the crippling affects of arthritis. While he stayed on his diet, he improved. Off the diet, he worsened. He was scared and would do anything to try to make his life better.

A funny thing was happening to Winston because of his condition. People started to treat him better than they had before, and they actually went out of their way to help him. He did not ask for the help, but there it was anytime he needed it. Winston began to need it more and more.

We talked about his condition and he told us the following story. He was once married and extremely miserable in the marriage. He was alone most of the time. He felt sorry for himself. Winston was watching television one night and he saw a commercial asking for donations to a charity for persons with a debilitating disease. He said to himself, "I wish I had something like that, then people wouldn't be so rotten to me."

As Winston told the story, he wept because he felt that was the reason for his arthritis. He really thought that he had caused the arthritis because of his negative, selfish thought. If you asked him today, Winston would probably still believe that.

But, that is not the point of the story. Winston began to deal with his disability in the usual ways. He became so unable to work that he was granted a leave to seek medical care for the arthritis. Winston could not work so he applied for disability benefits. He continued to use some alternative therapies because according to his arthritis specialist, there were no solutions except heavy doses of medication.

Winston's doctor scoffed at the idea that diet had anything to do with Winston's condition, and he was very upset because Winston had not gone ahead with the surgery.

Winston deteriorated rapidly following his job loss. He tried rehabilitation therapies because he needed "someone to push" him to do the things he consciously knew were good for him. He did not have the willpower to do it himself. There is that word again, "power." He did not have the power or the empowerment to do these things for himself.

Winston was different from other clients because he had already begun to believe that he could do what conventional medicine could not. He knew the answer was not there, but he did not go the one step further to explore his options in his own energy system.

He began to find his answers during a session with us in which he described his youth and responsibilities placed on him during that time. He was a very young boy when his parents demanded that he become the "father" of the family and take care of his younger brothers and sisters. This burden for a young child created an impression on Winston. This impression had followed him throughout his life. He could never get away from responsibilities which seemed too great to handle. Winston began to look for ways unconsciously to give up responsibility to others. He did it at work where he was truly responsible for large accounts and billing. He found himself slowing down at work, supposedly because of his physical limitations. In fact, he felt that the burden of responsibility for all that money was too great for him.

Winston went on to describe his personal responsibilities and the almost adolescent rebellion he felt at times trying to get away with doing little to help a relationship. He ran from relationship to relationship trying to find something which would shelter him as an adult. Nothing worked. The only thing that really did work was having a disability which would allow him to be a little less than his friends thought he could be. In this way, he did not have any responsibility to anyone. He could just not try and people still "loved" him. After a while this burden of responsibility took its toll on Winston and he found that life was not a happy situation. People became bored with helping him and he felt their rejection. It was time to move on and he did not know how.

It was at that point that Winston began to work on the answers. He recalled experiences in which responsibility was a theme, but he did not recall these experiences through talk therapy. He was taught how to actually link into his internal computer memory bank of experiences to find the answers. He "saw" various experiences of his life in which he learned a lesson about his self-worth. In each experience, he recognized the emotional attachment he had to the experience which had colored his lifetime.

In the present day and time, Winston actually altered the memory of the experience. In other words, he watched the scenes unfold and altered the outcome in his memory. He did not, or could not, change the event. The event would always stand as it was. The only thing he could change was the emotional interpretation of the event.

Winston learned that because he had been given responsibility in several situations, he felt failure every time he did not fulfill the obligations. What did this have to do with his arthritis? We are not saying that the arthritis will be reversed or changed by the recollection of past experiences. What we are saying is that Winston has found an empowerment now which will allow him to change his lifestyle. The empowerment will give him the opportunity to succeed where he once failed and the empowerment will lessen the imbalance in his life.

The imbalanced situation of his life has led to the stress in his life which led to the exacerbation of symptoms of the arthritis. He did not learn to manage his stress; he learned to balance his energy system emotionally and mentally so that the balance in his physical system was easier to achieve.

Winston has returned to a job for which he is well qualified. He still has some difficulty with his arthritic condition because there has been so much physical strain on his body from a lack of discipline and the deterioration of the soft tissue in his body. He must now begin the process of rebuilding the strength of this body so that he can then rebuild his life.

Winston will succeed because he is an achiever. Winston will succeed because he has empowered himself with knowledge about himself and he can use that empowerment to do anything he wishes. Stressful situations are no longer the reason to run into a cave and hide. Stress causes him to become more determined to find answers to the imbalance in his life and solve it.

Winston developed a self-trust and a self-responsibility that he had searched for all of his life. He was constantly attempting to do what others wanted to the denial of his own worth. Without someone telling him he was worth something or that he was loved, Winston could not be happy. He has learned a valuable lesson about loving oneself. By caring about himself, he can now begin the long road back to health and accomplishment. Accomplishment and achievement not measured by the standards of others, but rather by his own sense of confidence in himself.

LEADERS ARE EMPOWERED BY CHALLENGE

Warren Bennis and co-author Burt Nanus in their book about leaders titled, appropriately enough, LEADERS talk about the characteristics which ninety successful leaders shared. They concluded that these leaders viewed every false step or failure along the road to success as a learning opportunity and not the end of the world. Leaders achieve because of the challenges that come from stressful situations. And the power that comes from that stress can be used to succeed if a leader knows how to do that.

Bennis and Nanus view power as "the basic energy to initiate and sustain action translating intention into reality, the quality without which leaders cannot lead." The power which we feel comes from positive stress is the same power which has been identified by Bennis and Nanus in that they too say that "we are a nation suffering from a serious power blockage."

The power of self-esteem and the achievement of empowerment for yourself are the hallmarks of positive stress.

131

Whether you use that stress in physical, mental, or emotional ways to find that empowerment is not the point. The point is that empowerment can be achieved for yourself without someone else "giving" you any power. The people who are leaders are those who have a self-core which already senses that there is a power within them to change. The people who are leaders are those who approach their stress in particular and unique ways through their own energy systems. The empowerment which comes from that increased self-esteem can change ordinary lives into extraordinary adventures.

"The significant problems we face cannot be solved at the same level of thinking we were at when we created them."

Albert Einstein

EIGHT

THE POWER
OF THE 21ST CENTURY MIND

Robert Kennedy was one of those people who could move an audience just by the power of his presence and the energy with which he spoke his words. His energy and drive carried a generation along on a wave of hope and idealism until that day in California in 1968 when the wave of hope came crashing down around us all. He inspired us with his words about the future and the promise of that new future. His words have been used for years as inspiration for us all. One of his most often quoted remarks was actually inspired by the words of a man who lived in another generation.

George Bernard Shaw challenged his generation with the words, "You see things; and you say, 'Why?' But, I dream things that never were; and I say, 'Why not?'" The thought is there no matter who said it or who said it first. Kennedy and Shaw both challenged our ideas about the future. Instead of bemoaning the situations in which we find ourselves, these men urged us to dream a dream about a future which was equally as possible as the present.

We have discussed many ideas in these pages. Ideas born out of that very same question of Shaw's, posed many years ago. When we look to the future and to the 21st century just around the corner, we also ask, "Why not?" Why can't there be a turn around in the way we use our own power? Carl Jung said, "Your vision will become clear only when you look into your own heart. Who looks outside, dreams; who looks inside, awakes."

As we face the new century, we believe we must all look inside to make the outside a reality. This is the promise of the 21st century mind.

THE 21ST CENTURY MIND

The 21st century. For many of us that new century seemed completely out of sight in our youth. *The 21st century.* It sounded like something out of science fiction. To many of us, it still does. But, whether we accept it or not, the 21st century is upon us. The years of the future are not so far into the future anymore. *The 21st century.* It is here!

What does the 21st century mean to us? Is it a time of promise or apprehension? Is it a time of hope or dread? Do we look into its misty days like someone looking into the fog in the early morning? The days of the 21st century are certainly not clear to many of us. What kind of mind can comprehend and appreciate the promise of the future? What kind of mind must we have to look forward with hope?

That mind is the "21st century mind." This mind looks forward with confidence because the future is full of not just "hope" but "promise." The promise of the 21st century can be seen in the advances of the 20th century. When this century began almost 100 years ago, humans did not fly to other bodies in our solar system. Humans did not fly above the ground at supersonic speeds. Humans did not move around the planet in vehicles which approached speeds of 200 or 300 miles per hour on rails. *And*, humans did not speak to one another through airways or soundwaves. To see a moving picture in your own home sent from thousands of miles away was the dream of the visionaries and lunatics of the day.

We have seen these wondrous happenings, and many more, in only the last few decades as compared to the first five or six.

Humankind reached the moon 70 years after the century was born. Air transportation became common after almost 40 years had passed. Television became a part of everyone's home life almost 60 years into the 20th century. *Think of where we have come just in the last few years!*

But, along with advances, there have been some problems. We seem to have more wars breaking out in more places than at any other time in history. These wars threaten the very existence of the plant itself. The confidence of the planet's inhabitants is waning under the weight of struggles with the economy, as well as the pollution which threatens our air. Diseases of unspeakable proportions have become our daily terrors and our own brothers and sisters have become our possible enemies.

Humankind at the brink of a new century faces a complex future. Perhaps this will be the most complex in recorded or unrecorded history. The problems seem insurmountable and the possibilities seem infinite. Just when we think we have seen it all, we have not.

How are we to learn to cope with a future like no other generation has ever had to face? Who are the people who will lead us into the 21st century and secure our futures? Who indeed?

THE LEADERS OF THE 21ST CENTURY

The leaders of this paradoxical future are reading this book. The leaders of this future already know where they and we are going. The leaders among us do not look to the dawn of the 21st century. They are looking *beyond the dawn of the century.* They are looking to the mid-century. They are planning for a world most of us are still imagining in science fiction. The leaders of the next century must look for solutions to problems the likes of which most of us never imagined.

Why do we say that the leaders of the future are those who are reading this book? They have something in common. Without

135

an understanding of the energy system of every person living on this planet, we will continue to treat each other as numbers without feelings. We will continue to treat those of different color, sex, background, and creed as either superior to us or inferior to us. The racism, sexism, and nationalism of the present day will never change if we do not believe that each individual system shares something very basic with every other individual system. *That something is energy.*

This energy we are talking about is the same energy Naisbitt and Aburdene mention in MEGATRENDS 2000. "Individualism does recognize that individual energy matters. When people satisfy genuine achievement needs--in art, business, or science--society gains." (Naisbitt and Aburdene, page 299). They continue to say, as we look to the new century that "individuals everywhere feel empowered, freer to determine their own fate." (Naisbitt and Aburdene, page 301)

One of those new leaders is a man named Marty. He is the president of his own international marketing company. He began his business after being a sales director for a major manufacturing company. As a sales director, Marty had won the admiration of everyone in the company. He took the company literally from the bottom of the market to the top of the market in a short period of time and in a recession!

He worked hard for his company and the management team whom he respected. The years passed and Marty believed, without reservation, that his position in the company would be there for as long as he wished. Over the years, he had gained a good reputation in international circles as a company representative. The future looked very bright. Marty's energy was wrapped up in the company's success or failure. His energy and the energy of the company were so enmeshed that if there was a change in one there would most certainly be a change in the other.

So, what led him to leave such a position and start out on his own? You guessed it. *New management. New energy.* The old guard of the company was being forced out in a hostile takeover, and Marty was faced with new people running the company. These new people were not those whom Marty respected and he had many disagreements with the new management over the next few weeks.

Marty could not believe the directions that the company was taking. Suddenly, the management was no longer aware of the contributions of Marty or people like him who had devoted their lives to the success of the company. Regardless of this fact, he was a good manager and continued to do his best under the circumstances. In other words, he kept his mouth shut and did not do anything to disrupt the company's policies.

Months passed. Marty found himself being placed in many compromising situations. His new managers expected him to do things which he felt were unethical, and he refused. Every refusal caused more tension between him and the company management. Marty could not compromise himself, and the company could not tolerate anyone around who was not absolutely loyal.

Marty walked into his office one day to find that his files had been opened. He questioned his secretary, but she denied any knowledge of who had been in the office. Although he did not notice anything missing, he did feel "violated". He immediately went to his boss and asked why his office files had been searched. Of course, the boss "knew nothing" about the incident and implied that Marty was perhaps paranoid.

Marty was good at his job, but being good at a job was not enough. He soon learned that the mission of his new bosses was very focused. Marty was in their way. He was too tied to the old management and the new management wanted to get rid of him.

One day, while Marty was out on a sales trip for the company, news came to him that he was being sued by the company for stealing files. Marty was shocked by this new piece of treachery. He felt the company's management wanted him to get *permanently lost,* but he never dreamed that they would sink to such depths to force him out of his position.

Marty returned home that night to find that not only had he been sued unfairly, but he did not even have a job! He tried to contact the office and speak to his boss, but no one was available for him. He didn't expect to talk with anyone, but he had to try. Marty contacted his attorney and began a long journey to a miserable confrontation.

Marty's old company was not going to play by the rules. Whatever Marty represented to them, they didn't like it and they wanted it "eliminated". He was almost powerless to fight the company. After years of faithful service, he found that even old friends and co-workers could not speak to him. He felt cut off and alone.

ENERGY FOR CHANGE

Energy is the basis of life on this planet and perhaps beyond this planet. The physicists have pronounced over the years that there are two physical realities. Those are matter and energy. Matter is the substance we can see and which is tangible for us. Energy is something most of us cannot see, but we know that it exists. Do you ever see "electricity?" Not the *result* of the electricity, but the actual "*electricity*" itself. Did you ever "see" x-rays or any radiating energy at all? Yes, we can see the result of energy, but most of us cannot see the energy itself.

The energy working within Marty was the energy of emotion and thought. This form of energy is as intangible as other forms of energy. We know that electricity exists even though we don't see it. All we really need to know is that when we turn on the lamps on our desks, they will light. We don't have to see the energy to know it exists. The electricity of our bodies is much the same. We can see the *result* of our thinking process. We don't have to see it to know that it exists. "Seeing" our nerve impulses is not necessary. For most of us! *To know that we can think is very important.*

That is what the 21st century mind can do. *It can think.* Seems rather simple, doesn't it? The mind can think, can't it? Yours does all the time, right? Well, maybe not all the time, but most of the time. The mind thinks. That is its function. But, we are not

138

talking about simple thinking. We are talking about thinking with a capital "T". The mind of the future must learn, interpret, assimilate, and create its own realities from the raw materials it has available to it. The 21st century will demand that thinking is vital to the survival of the entire population. It is the energy of this thinking process which is vital to our existence as a species.

COMPLETE CAPACITY FOR CHANGE

The 21st century mind must be used to its fullest capacity. When we speak of capacity, we are referring to the "complete capacity for change". In his book, the EXECUTIVE ODYSSEY, Frederick Harmon talks about the "complete act." The "complete act" is described as a mental, physical, and emotional combination which an executive leader must use in order to accomplish his or her personal best. (Harmon, page 24). When we talk about "complete capacity" in Energy Dynamics^R, we are talking about this comprehensive combination of physical, emotional, and mental power which can be used to accomplish whatever is needed or whatever is desired.

Let's go back to Marty and his 21st century mind. Marty's major problem with the company came from the uncomfortable position in which he found himself. He knew that he had done nothing wrong, but he could not prove it. Like many of us, he never felt that there was anything from which he needed protection because he always dealt with people honestly. It was not his nature to distrust. When you do not believe that you must be cautious, you are rarely prepared. This is the position in which Marty found himself.

After years of service, he found that those whom he trusted were lying to him. He discovered that old friends had told stories about him that were not only untrue, but defaming. Marty could only wait for the next slander and the next threat. He could do nothing but wait for "his day in court" to fight back.

He waited. *He waited.* Through months of legal maneuvering and through months of depositions and counterattacks, Marty kept his own counsel and tried ways to survive.

Leaders share many characteristics. One characteristic is the capacity to take advantage of every tool at their disposal. To use everything necessary to accomplish the impossible is one of the hallmarks of the true leader in business or in any profession. The leader of the 21st century will be the woman or man who will take the energy of this comprehensive capacity and use it to best advantage.

LEADERSHIP CAPACITY

A leader of the 21st century must not only take advantage of every tool he or she has, but must also be judicious in the use of the tool. In other words, to use your own energy system well is not enough. In our complex community of humankind, we must all be aware of the effect we all have individually upon others. There are many people who have gone through courses, retreats, and programs to develop personal self-confidence, self-empowerment, and self-worth. We as a society read massive volumes of books on self-help and "pop psychology." We buy endless amounts of audio and video tapes for the purpose of finding answers to some very basic questions.

What is the meaning of life? Where did I come from? *Where am I going?* How do I find myself? *How do I rid myself of guilt?* How do I learn to love? What is unconditional love? How do I find my power? All of these questions and hundreds more run through our minds as we grow, think, change, and search. We all have these questions from time to time and most of us want some answers. We seek out those wiser than we to give us the answers. We look for the "magic" pill or the "magic" formula to create a fulfilled life. Do we find it?

If we had found it, there would be no more market for self-help books, personal growth tapes, and seminars in self-worth.

Richard Bach, in his book, ILLUSIONS, says it best. "Here is a test to find whether your mission on earth is finished; if you're alive, it isn't." If you are still alive and searching for answers, then perhaps Mr. Bach is correct. Your purpose on this earth is not finished. In the 21st century, the answers to these questions will either be much clearer or much more vague. Will the future give us answers or will the future just give us more questions?

Marty's purpose on earth was rather vague after he was discharged from his old company. He was asking himself many of the questions we ask ourselves every day, but he did have the advantage of being a leader with a capacity for change. Marty knew certain things about himself. He knew that he had done no wrong. He knew that the company to which he had given so many of his years had abandoned him and had wished him ill. The reasons for this were not clear to Marty, and perhaps they weren't even relevant. Marty had to start life over again with a new set of rules.

Connie Mack once said, "You can't win any game unless you are ready to win." Marty was ready to win. Marty began by examining his life purpose. Through a confidential one-on-one coaching, Marty began to rebuild his confidence and his life. As with most executives, Marty had learned through the years to repress his emotions at the job and hide the anger, frustration, fear, and stress he had known. Of course, he always had these emotions, but they just were not talked about with anyone!

Marty had learned that to be a professional, one had to learn to act professionally and to act competently. One of our clients says it this way: "Always act sincere, even if you don't mean it." Marty knew this well. He had spent a lifetime learning to behave in the way that was *expected*. He did not discuss emotional responses about work with anyone.

The emotions were there of course, but there was neither the time nor the place to vent them. Marty had many emotional responses now. He had so many he didn't recognize them. He experienced physical symptoms at first. He had headaches, stomachaches, backaches, and a myriad of complaints. He was losing sleep and eating too much. He was snapping at his wife. He was hiding out from friends. He was becoming withdrawn. He was working hard to start a new life, but he felt sabotaged everywhere he turned.

Mark Twain warned us about only taking academic wisdom from any experience "lest we be like the cat that sits down on a hot stove lid. She will never sit down on a hot stove lid again, and that is well; but also she will never sit down on a cold one any more." If we are afraid of the experience and only learn from it mentally, the lesson of that experience will be lost. Marty had to be careful that the bitterness he felt over his situation and the experience did not color his whole world. The development of your own power comes from taking the positive from any experience and using it well. The mind which can do that is the mind which can move into the future with new power and new possibility. Marty had such a mind.

Even with all of the adversity he had experienced, Marty had a leader's capacity to learn from his experience. It was not easy, but in order to continue to be a successful businessman and a successful person, he moved on.

ENERGY DYNAMICS^R AND LEADERSHIP

Energy Dynamics^R gives us an opportunity to learn, to grow, and to develop. The understanding of our energy systems and, more importantly, the monitoring of those systems are the pivot points upon which we believe the 21st century mind is built. We must begin to use the power we have to change and succeed. We must learn to listen to our own systems. We must begin to develop the 21st century mind today.

Marty first began to develop his 21st century mind by learning about stress. Marty had always believed that stress was a necessary evil and that, at most, it was a temporary condition that could be handled. He worked out and exercised to relieve the stress. He ate to relieve the stress. He never really felt that the physical and emotional symptoms he was having were "stress-response symptoms."

Marty is an extremely intelligent, competent, and well-rounded man who was not born yesterday. He "knew" at some level that stress existed, but he did not know what to do about it. Nor, did he realize that stress was just a signal of some deeper problems with which he must deal.

He tackled the physical symptoms first. Insomnia was one thing that Marty *did not need*. Being deprived of sleep led to more serious problems. He could hardly begin a new business without regular rest from time to time. The insomnia had sent him to his family doctor for tranquilizers. These worked for a while and then, he was not only tired, but also foggy. Tranquilizers were not the answer.

Hard work was not the answer either for Marty. The harder he worked, the more he needed the rest he was not getting. It was a vicious cycle from which he could not escape. As the months wore on, Marty finally began to look for answers in the past. He chose to begin with his feelings of rejection.

Through several coaching sessions, Marty learned that although he appeared to "have it all," he had never felt that he was successful. He always felt like that little boy from the wrong side of the tracks who had become successful almost by a fluke. His old impressions of desperately trying to prove himself were deeply embedded in the past. These old impressions were so much a part of Marty, he was not consciously aware of them. As with all impressions stored in the memory, these feelings of inferiority were on an unconscious level, and Marty did not realize how powerful they had become.

Through the program, he was able to recall many incidents in which he had taken an easy way out of a situation. There were many times in his life when he had avoided conflict by playing the game according to someone else's rules. Marty had been successful, but he had been successful at someone else's game. He had to make his own game now, if he was to survive.

He began his own game of which he was the director and he started the long road toward achievement. His new game began with a recognition that ultimately he had to satisfy himself. He could no longer work to be the reflection of what his company wanted him to be. He could no longer be the reflection of what his parents had wanted. Marty could no longer be the reflection of what his wife wanted. He had tried for years to please everyone's idea of what and who he should be. It was time to stop.

In order to stop, Marty had to rearrange his view of himself. Very few of us really know who we are and if we do glimpse some aspect of that true self, we sometimes hide from its discovery. Marty glimpsed aspects of himself he had never seen before. He began to like what he saw and he gave himself permission to be more than others expected him to be.

It was very rough going for Marty and his loved ones. Marty's friends, family, and wife were forced to deal with a new person. The biggest threat to Marty's new "persona" was that others could not believe that he could stand alone without the company behind him. This was the first thing Marty had to believe and the first thing those around him had to accept.

Marty had learned something about himself that very few ever do. He had learned that deep inside there was a person he could actually like and love. Regardless of the love of others, Marty knew that he was worthy of love. True self-worth is just that. Knowing that you are worthy of respect, love, and friendship. Marty had to learn to love himself. *For the first time in his life.* Marty did not feel love reflected back to him from other people, he actually felt the love inside that didn't need anyone else.

LOVE, ACCEPTANCE, AND RESPECT

Love is a powerful reflection of the energy system at work in the mental and emotional realm. The energy of love is something which fires the 21st century mind. We have gone from fighting for others and imposing our wills upon others in the past decades to the new paradigm of trying to become individuals with our own power.

Into the 21st century, men and women like Marty will have the opportunity for a new power. Naisbitt and Aburdene look to the future of this global world in MEGATRENDS 2000 to say that "throughout history, power has been associated with institutions, with physical and military power . . . People felt powerless against their social context. The only way they could assert themselves was by opposing tradition, by tearing down what was no longer useful." (Naisbitt and Aburdene, page 309).

There is a new possibility today. "The individual can influence reality by identifying the directions in which society is headed. Knowledge is power, it has often been said. Even if you do not endorse the directions of trends, you are empowered by your knowledge about it." (Naisbitt and Aburdene, page 309). Marty and other 21st century minds take what they have been given through knowledge of themselves and their situations and use that knowledge for power.

Marty had to accept himself for himself. When he could do that, all things were possible. *Marty changed his diet.* His wife had urged him to do that for years, but Marty changed his diet *because he had made the decision!* Marty started his own business. His old clients had been telling him to do that for years. Marty made his own decision. *Marty had made decisions about his life, probably for the first time in his life.*

To this day, Marty is still battling the old battles, but there is a very important difference. No longer is his success or failure a result of what others believe him to be. Marty judges whether he is a success or not. Sometimes those successes are not what we think they "should" be, but if there is a *conscious decision to act,* that is a success.

William James cautions us that *"when you have to make a choice and don't make it, that is in itself a choice."* Marty is a successful, excited, fulfilled, and confident person who has faced demons that most of us never will. He has traveled from desperation to helplessness to empowerment. He has just begun.

THE SHIFTING PARADIGM OF LEADERSHIP

The shifting paradigms of the new century cross the lines of business and personal lives. The challenges of the future in our global marketplace make it imperative that the new leaders take the stresses of this new world and use those positively. Over the years we have been privileged to observe changes in the perceptions of many people. All of these "leaders" in their own ways have "shifted their paradigms" of success and achievement by harnessing the challenges of professional and personal life. This shift in perception has given each of them the power which only comes from knowing your own mind and energy system.

Patricia Aburdene, in her landmark book MEGATRENDS FOR WOMEN written with her partner, John Naisbitt, says, "Fifty years from now, when that ideal is realized (the ideal of a partnership society) . . . it will be clear in retrospect that the *turning point*, the time when the critical mass for social transformation was present, occurred in the decade of the 1990's." (Aburdene and Naisbitt, p. 326)

The 21st century mind has the ability to change perspective. Emotional perspectives are challenged every day in some way and those challenges can lead to discoveries. Those discoveries make us strong and make the future bright.

One of the most remarkable women of the 20th century worked alongside her husband during a depression, a world war, and a major illness. She said that her strength came from somewhere inside her and from her upbringing. We believe there was something more to Eleanor Roosevelt than "upbringing." One of our clients was a woman whose husband was involved with the fledgling unions of the 1930's. As a result of her husband's fame and importance, she was honored to be invited to the White House to have lunch with Mrs. Roosevelt.

146

Mrs. Roosevelt was a perfect hostess, and the aspect that impressed our client was the focus of this woman who appeared to have survived great tragedy, but had risen above it by some unseen strength. Mrs. Roosevelt has been quoted as saying that "you gain strength, courage, and confidence by every experience in which you really stop to look fear in the face. You are able to say to yourself, "I lived through this horror. I can take the next thing that comes along." You must do the thing you think you cannot do."

We have outlined a version of the 21st century mind which runs the gamut from executive to career woman to George Bernard Shaw. At first glance all of these examples of what we call the use of stress to direct empowerment seem to have little in common. But, the common element here is that each of these people recognized that out of stressful situations comes a certain energy which when used positively can bring about great power. This power allows the individual to make sweeping changes or subtle changes. The choice is for that person to make.

Many of our seminars are designed specifically for those who either own their own businesses or who manage businesses. In all of our training seminars and our private counseling, there is one theme. *The use of stress for power or empowerment through the energy system.* The positive use of stress can be an empowering tool for anyone who has the "self-core" to recognize it. Anyone in whatever walk of life benefits from an increase in power and confidence, but the stress we find among managers in the 1990's is crucial to personal and professional success and leadership. As we move into a new century, the old rules won't work anymore. The world is much smaller than it once was. Men and women in business struggle with a communication avalanche today unforeseen by our grandparents and parents.

In order to survive and thrive in the 21st century, the stresses caused by this future must be turned into assets. We have told you many personal stories of ordinary people who have challenged themselves, and us, to find answers to questions many people ask.

How do I make my life a success? How can I survive the pressures of my life? Can I survive the pressures of my life?

Think Bite #9

Because you are developing the 21st century mind, let's think about the future. What are the goals you have to accomplish? What is the dream of your future? Take a moment to sit down and write those goals, but let's do it a little differently than you may have in the past.

Before you think of them, try this experiment. Think of one of the *most pessimistic persons you have ever known.* You may have to go back to childhood or maybe, just back to work. Think about that person for a few minutes and remember how negative he or she is.

Now, after you think carefully about that person, write down all of your future goals. What do you want to accomplish in your future? In your 21st century?

Got the list? Was it hard to do? *Are you confident right now that you can accomplish all you have listed?*

Let's move on. Take another deep breath, pause, and now, think about the most important person in your life. The one person above all *you admire and love the most.* Concentrate on that person and why he or she means so much to you.

"Back to the future", and another sheet of paper. Write down your goals for the future. Where do you want to be and what will you be doing in the 21st century? Look at that list. *Do you have confidence that you will accomplish those goals?*

Did you notice any difference between the first and second list? Was one list harder to write that the other? Do you know why? When your mind is occupied with a negative image or thought, it is more difficult to concentrate and accomplish anything positive. With a good thought and some positive feeling in your system, the job is easier. Remember this the next time you have a project to complete which requires a great deal of self-confidence.

Michel De Saint-Pierre said, "An optimist may see a light where there is none, but why must the pessimist always run to blow it out?" Just so those people for whom you have negative thoughts. *Why let those thoughts cause you to blow out the light of your future?* Remember the 21st century mind will always seek new possibilities and will change the accepted paradigms.

THE DYNAMICS OF ACHIEVEMENT AND SUCCESS

Whether it is a corporate executive in a major city struggling with multi-million dollar quarterly losses or a widowed woman struggling to start a new life without her husband or a psychologist trying to find answers to her own personal dilemmas, the dynamics are all the same. The details may change, but the theme is the same. We all come into this world alone. We live lives in which we interact with other people, we love other people, we hate other people, and we fear other people. During your life, the "bottom-line" truth is that no matter what persons you meet, what deals you make, or how much money you possess, you are ultimately going to do it alone.

But, wait a minute, that's not bad. If you choose, you can empower your own life to turn the stress, disappointment, and the experiences of living into success, accomplishment, and achievement.

Sometimes, the conventional wisdom tells us that what you want, you cannot have. And what you expect to happen, won't. There seem to be people out there who are always ready to say, "Yes, but THEY SAY . . ." "They say" a great many things. "They say" that success comes only to the fortunate. "They say" that power is corrupting. "They say" that stress is a negative scourge upon humankind. "They say" that there are some things which are beyond our control. Maybe so, *but. . .*

Reuben Ross Holmes spent 7 months of his life in an intensive care unit before his death. For 7 months, his family and his friends watched the giant medical machine care for, support, and control his life. For many people having someone in the hospital means that you have no control over the care he or she receives. "They say" nurses, doctors, aids, and support personnel in hospitals take care of everything and the family must stand by and watch. Everything is out of your control. They say, *but. . .*

When Reuben went to the hospital, he was a number as many patients are. As a matter of fact, it can be no other way given the massive volume of patients hospitals handle. The care is efficient, but mechanical. Compassionate, but impersonal. As the weeks passed, this situation changed. Not by any overt means, but by the quiet determination of a core of friends and family who empowered themselves to be partners in Reuben's care. The family and friends were given permission by the hospital to visit him at odd hours and to take over many of the chores which "they say" family members cannot do.

There was a constant stream of visitors to Reuben who read to him, talked with him, encouraged him, and supported him. This man was completely silent, but his wishes were granted by family and friends with no verbal communication. Over time, we noticed an interesting thing happening. The nurses in whose charge he had been placed began to refer to him *not as a number in a bed, but as a man with a name.* One early morning, we overheard a report being dictated by one of his nurses. The young man was giving details about the three patients he had cared for during the night. "Bed 10 was very restless last night." "Bed 8 was comfortable and all medications were given as scheduled." *"Reuben had a good night."* Actually, he was in Bed 14. They don't call the thirteenth bed in intensive care Bed 13. Reuben had become a real person to his caretakers. The power of this stressful lifestyle his family and friends had lived had turned this man into an identifiable person.

"They say" nurses don't have time to know their patients and they steel themselves from emotional contact. But, sometimes the caretakers *really do care.* In the 21st century, let's hope that the power of disease and illness can be turned into an asset to teach us to look at each other with personal compassion.

The power of disease and illness is just one of the powers in the world today. The stress of living in the 20th century can be turned into a extraordinary opportunity and challenge for the 21st century and beyond. Stephen Covey says "paradigms are powerful because they create the lens through which we see the world. The power of the paradigm shift is the essential power of quantum change, whether that shift is an instantaneous or a slow and deliberate process." (Covey, 7 HABITS OF HIGHLY EFFECTIVE PEOPLE, page 32)

The people whose stories you have read all faced a shift in their perceptions of their own lives and the lives of others. Whether that shift was in career, personal life, or relationships, there was a change brought about by stress. In every case of a successful shift to positive stress, the person found new power to move into a new perspective or a new "paradigm." The old ways of viewing the world do not work anymore. The leaders of the world of the 21st century will be those ordinary and extraordinary people who have a self-core which pushes them on to find their own power, *a power that comes from the positive use of stress.* This is the positive stress factor and this is the future.

151

"In the last analysis it is our conception of death which decides our answers to all the questions that life puts to us."

Dag Hammarskjold

EPILOGUE

In the early moments of Sunday, February 10, 1991, my dear friend, Marcel Joseph Vogel suffered a heart attack. Despite all efforts, he did not survive the attack and his spirit left the body he had occupied for almost 74 years. His death was without pain and swift. His last day was spent taking pictures at his grandson's birthday dinner.

The death of this loving man came at a strangely appropriate season--a time of warmth and love with St. Valentine's Day and a time of divine love and sacrifice at Easter culminating in the celebration of the resurrection and the promise of eternal life.

Marcel's life was molded with his loves--his love of mary, his wife, his love of the Church, his love of family and friends, and his lifelong love of his work. He wore his loves like a great cloak of many hues and yards of experience falling in huge folds around him. This cloak was threadbare with rejections, disillusion, and disappointment, but it was also made strong by faith and trust.

It was not long after I met Marcel that he showed me a dollhouse he and Mary shared and I marveled at the loving detail of each tiny piece. He told me that when his wife was away, he would sit for hours and study this dollhouse and it brought her closer to him. Now, that he is "away" the memory of those tiny pieces of our time together bring him closer to me.

As I became enveloped in Marcel's world, I often would find that I needed not to speak because there was a communication that went beyond words. We had known each other long before we met and his big bear hugs carried me through many trials and personal triumphs. Marcel was my mentor, confidante, and taskmaster, my brother, my father, and my son. The times we spent together were precious and full of wonder. He always allowed me to discover truths he could have told me, but waited until I had learned and shared the learning with him, and then, resting his great head back against his favorite chair would say, "Now, you know." It often frustrated me that he could have easily saved so much time by just telling me what

I needed to learn, but he knew that I did not need to be told. He trusted me more than I trusted myself. And so, I learned.

There was so much yet to share and learn together, but I remember something Marcel told me after my father died. He shared the experience of his own father's death and the thought that his father was still with him after death, guiding and teaching. He said to me, "Your father can help you more now than when he was on Earth and you will feel him near you."

Marcel will always be "near" me and he will teach me again and again, perhaps even more now, without the limits of time and distance. His cloak of love and the joy of his living will surround me wherever I go and I will carry his love to those I meet.

When last we spoke, I told him that I was ready to do whatever was needed to help him in his life's work. Tears welled in his eyes and he thanked me. He said he knew I was ready and said, "Now, you know."

Marcel was buried on St. Valentine's Day near his beloved San Francisco, wearing the robe of a Third Order Dominican as he had requested, carrying a healing crystal *and* a rosary, with a teddy bear for company on his journey.

Now, I know.

Rebecca
February 27, 1991

*"Live long
and
prosper."*

Mr. Spock
Star Trek

REFERENCES

Aburdene, Patricia and John Naisbitt. *Megatrends for Women.* New York: Villard Books, 1992.

Bach, Richard. *Illusions.* Delacorte Press, 1977.

Bennis, Warren and Burt Nanus. *Leaders: The Strategies for Taking Charge.* New York: Harper & Row, 1985.

Covey, Stephen R. *The Seven Habits of Highly Effective People: Restoring the Character Ethic.* New York: Simon and Schuster, 1989.

Decker, Bert. *You've Got to Be Believed to Be Heard.* New York: St. Martin's Press, 1992.

Edwards, Anne. *A Remarkable Woman: A Biography of Katharine Hepburn.* New York: William Morrow and Company, Inc., 1985.

Harmon, Frederick G. *The Executive Odyssey: Secrets of a Career Without Limits.* New York: John Wiley & Sons, 1989.

John-Roger and Peter McWilliams. *Do It!: Let's Get Off Our Buts.* Los Angeles: Prelude Press, 1991.

John-Roger and Peter McWilliams. *You Can't Afford the Luxury of a Negative Thought.* Los Angeles: Prelude Press, 1989.

Kouzes, James M. and Barry Z. Posner. *The Leadership Challenge: How to Get Extraordinary Things Done in Organizations.* San Francisco: Jossey-Bass Publishers, 1987.

Naisbitt, John and Patricia Aburdene. *Megatrends 2000: Ten New Directions for the 1990's*. New York: William Morrow and Company, Inc., 1990.

Popcorn, Faith. *The Popcorn Report: Faith Popcorn on the Future of Your Company, Your World, Your Life*. New York: Doubleday, 1991.

Satir, Virginia. *The New Peoplemaking*. Mountain View, California: Science and Behavior Books, Inc., 1988.

Tompkins, Peter and Christopher Bird. *The Secret Life of Plants*. New York: Harper & Row, 1973.

Travis, John W., M.D. and Regina Sara Ryan. *The Wellness Workbook*. Berkeley, California: Ten Speed Press, 1988.

INDEX

Aburdene, Patricia, 136, 145-146

achievement, 5, 11, 29-30, 36, 40-41, 58, 64, 111, 121, 131, 136, 144, 146

arthritis, 127-128, 130

Bach, Richard, 141

balance, 9-10, 24, 31-34, 36, 53-54, 66, 72-73, 79-81, 83-84, 93, 98, 103

Bennis, Warren, 131

Blake, William, 118

brain, 12, 30-33, 41, 47-50, 56, 61-62, 68-70, 88-89, 97

breath, 1, 9-10, 32-33, 47, 54-55, 77, 88, 148

bulimia, 70

caffeine, 80

Camus, Albert, 125

chocolate, 73, 78

Chronic Fatigue Snydrome, 112

Chronic Pain Syndrome, 47

communication, 13, 31-33, 41, 56, 147, 150

Covey, Stephen R., 113, 151

Decker, Bert, 41, 89

DeJarnette, Major Bertrand, 13-14

"Dynamic Tension", 41, 55

Einstein, Albert, 28

electricity, 7-8

Emerson, Ralph Waldo, 124

empower, 2-3, 16, 18, 64, 108, 113-115, 118, 120, 131, 136, 145, 149-150

empowerment, 16, 18, 48, 63-64, 108-110, 113, 115, 120, 129-132, 140, 146-148

"energy bucket", 86-88

Energy Dynamics^R, 4-6, 13, 17, 22, 38, 44-45, 47-51, 53, 56-58, 63-64, 75, 81, 83, 89, 92, 104, 107, 115-116, 122

energy level, 31

energy system, 3-4, 6, 8-9, 11-15, 18-22, 31-34, 42, 45-47, 49-51, 53, 56, 59-61, 62-65, 68-69, 72, 74-78, 81-84, 86, 89, 92-93, 97-98, 100, 103-104, 106, 110, 113, 118-120, 124-127, 129-130, 132, 136, 140, 142, 144, 146-147

Executive Odyssey, The, 36, 139

fear, 17, 58-59, 64-65, 82,
    88, 100-102, 107,
    121-123, 141, 147,
    149
"First Brain", 41, 89

Harmon, Frederick, 36, 139
Healing Brain, The, 30
Hepburn, Katharine, 24, 33
Hildebrand, Kenneth, 35
Holmes, Helen D., 108-110
Holmes, Oliver Wendell Jr.,
    22
Holmes, Rebecca Jo, 4, 108,
    119, 124
Holmes, Reuben Ross, 3, 150

image, 24, 27-28, 51, 67,
    71-72, 107
imagination, 28
impression(s), 15, 18, 22,
    24, 47, 86-92, 94-98,
    100, 102-107, 113, 122,
    125, 129, 143
Illusions, 141

journal writing, 119-120
Jung, Carl, 13, 114, 134

Karate Kid, The, 54
Kennedy, Robert, 133
Kouzes, James M., 44
Kreiger, Dolores, 13

leader(s), 26, 35, 41,
    44-45, 53, 111, 131-132,
    135-136, 139-142, 146,
    151
Leaders, 131

leadership, 41, 44, 140, 142,
    146-147
Leadership Challenge, The, 44

Maslow, Abraham, 25
massage, 112, 127
Megatrends for Women, 146
Megatrends 2000, 136, 145
memory, 1, 22, 30, 50-51, 56,
    59-60, 68-69, 71, 73,
    87-94, 97-105, 130, 143
mind, 4, 7-8, 15, 27-29, 31-33,
    39-40, 46-50, 60-61, 72,
    74, 77, 82-83, 90-91,
    93-94, 115-116, 124,
    134, 138-140, 142,
    144-149
Myers-Briggs Type
    Indicator™, 20

Naisbitt, John, 136, 145-146
New Peoplemaking, The, 53
New World, New Mind, 22
nutrition, 65-68, 80-81, 83-84

On Golden Pond, 24
Ornstein, Robert, 22, 30

paradigm(s), 145-146, 149, 151
Peale, Norman Vincent, 64
Perls, Fritz, 13
Popcorn, Faith, 111
Popcorn Report, The, 111
Pope John XXIII, 115
"positive stress", 3-5, 11-13,
    22, 44, 49, 60, 63-64,
    105, 120, 131, 151
positive thinking, 64, 88

power, 1, 3-4, 6-9, 11-13,
    15-16, 18, 20, 24,
    28-30, 32, 36, 40-43,
    48, 53-56, 61-62, 64,
    74, 77, 85, 87, 95-96,
    98, 100-101, 105-108,
    110, 112-116, 118-120,
    122-127, 129, 131-133,
    138-140, 142-147,
    149-151
"power plant", 7-8, 12
"prime directive", 49, 61, 63,
    68-70, 97

relaxation, 26-29, 36, 42, 55
Remarkable Woman, A, 23
Roosevelt, Eleanor, 146-147

*7 Habits of Highly Effective
    People*, 113, 151
Satir, Virgina, 53
Secret Life of Plants, The, 14
"self-core", 44-45, 47-48, 53,
    56, 108, 112, 132, 147,
    151
self-esteem, 18, 71, 108,
    110-116, 121, 123-125,
    131
Selye, Hans, 13
Shaw, George Bernard, 133,
    147
silence, 1-3
Stoppard, Miriam, 31
Streisand, Barbra, 58, 91-92
"stress point(s)", 37, 77

success, 5-6, 11-12, 23, 25,
    29, 35, 41, 44-45, 52,
    63-64, 70-71, 81-82,
    93, 95, 102, 117,
    120-122, 131, 136-137,
    142-143, 145-147, 149,
    151

21st century, 133-135, 138-142,
    144-149, 151
Think Bites, 9, 28, 37, 54, 77,
    79, 87, 119, 148
Travis, John, 11
Trump, Donald, 29
"tumbleweed", 56-57, 64
"tumbleweed people", 46, 56-57
Twain, Mark, 7, 114, 142

visualization, 27
Vogel, Marcel, 13-15, 24,
    48-49, 119, Epilogue

Wachner, Linda, 35
Webb, John Lee, 105
Webb, Marie, 113-115
Webb, Mary Lee, 4, 105, 107,
    114, 125-126
Wellness Workbook, 11

Yoda, 40, 88
*You've Got to Be Believed to
    Be Heard*, 41

SELECTED BIBLIOGRAPHY

Barker, Joel Arthur. *Paradigms: The Business of Discovering the Future*. New York: HarperCollins Publishers, 1992.

Barrentine, Pat, ed. *When the Canary Stops Singing: Women's Perspectives on Transforming Business*. San Francisco: Berrett-Koehler Publishers, 1993.

Belasco, James A. and Ralph C. Stayer. *Flight of the Buffalo: Soaring to Excellence, Learning to Let Employees Lead*. New York: Time Warner Books, Inc, 1993.

Benton, D.A. *Lions Don't Need to Roar*. New York: Warner Books, Inc., 1992.

Buzan, Tony with Barry Buzan. *The Mind Map Book^R*. London: BBC Books, 1993.

Collins, James C. and William C. Lazier. *Beyond Entrepreneurship: Turning Your Business Into an Enduring Great Company*. Englewood Cliffs, New Jersey: Prentice Hall, 1992.

Godfrey, Joline. *Our Wildest Dreams: Women Entrepreneurs Making Money, Having Fun, Doing Good*. New York: HarperCollins Publishers, Inc., 1992.

John-Roger and Peter McWilliams. *Wealth 101: Getting What You Want--Enjoying What You've Got*. Los Angeles: Prelude Press, 1992.

Kouzes, James M. and Barry Z. Posner. *Credibility: How Leaders Gain and Lost It, Why People Demand It*. San Francisco: Jossey-Bass Publishers, 1993.

McNally, David. *Even Eagles Need a Push: Learning to Soar in a Changing World*. Eden Prarie, Minnesota: TransForm Press, 1990.

Marinaccio, Dave. *All I Really Need to Know I Learned from Watching Star Trek*. New York: Crown Publishers, Inc., 1994.

Naisbitt, John. *Global Paradox: The Bigger the World Economy, the More Powerful its Smallest Players*. New York: William Morrow and Company, Inc., 1994.

Roddick, Anita. *Body and Soul*. New York: Crown Publishers, Inc., 1991.